Praise for *Successful Synagogue Fundraising Today: Overcoming the Fear of Asking for Money*

"Pushes congregational leaders to reframe the way we think about members and membership.... A thoughtful and wonderfully user-friendly contribution to a growing and necessary conversation."
 —**Rabbi B. Elka Abrahamson**, president, Wexner Foundation

"As a former synagogue rabbi, this book resonates strongly with the challenges I faced.... Helps [us] understand the principles of fundraising and development."
 —**Rabbi Asher Lopatin**, president, Yeshivat Chovevei Torah Rabbinical School

"Should be required reading for all synagogue leadership, from committee members to board members to temple presidents. It is fundraising 101 and so much more."
 —**Jodi Hessel**, past president, Temple Beth Am, Pinecrest (Miami), Florida

"A relationship-oriented, stewardship-driven approach to fundraising."
 —**Rabbi Deborah Waxman, PhD**, president, Reconstructionist Rabbinical College

"Of immense practical value.... David Mersky's insights into the theory and process of development enabled me, my lay leadership and staff to achieve success beyond our expectations."
 —**Rabbi Joshua M. Davidson**, senior rabbi, Congregation Emanu-El of the City of New York

"A great resource for every synagogue seeking to move from a culture of fundraisers to a culture of philanthropy that ... engages life-long donors. A comprehensive primer."
 —**Margo Gold**, international president, United Synagogue of Conservative Judaism

"A must-read for synagogue boards, clergy and staff."
 —**Dr. Ron Wolfson**, Fingerhut Professor of Education, American Jewish University; author, *Relational Judaism: Using the Power of Relationships to Transform the Jewish Community*

T0125905

Who Should Read This Book?

This book is for all of you who value the synagogue in your personal life—clergy, educators, staff, and, above all, the volunteers charged with the sacred task of sustaining Jewish life. In Shabbat 118b, the Talmud teaches that Rabbi Yossi said, "May my portion be with those who raise *tzedakah* and not with those who only distribute it."

In this book, we will explore what a comprehensive development and fundraising program can help you achieve. You will learn:

- How to engage the members of your congregation
- The difference between a High Holiday appeal and an annual fund program (and the value of the latter)
- How to create and execute an annual development plan
- Who will lead the development and fundraising effort
- The roles of volunteer leaders, clergy, and professional staff
- The habits of a highly successful fundraiser
- Where to find and how to learn about your prospective donors
- How to make the case for support of your congregation
- How to create a culture of asking
- The value of developing a strategy for each prospective donor
- How to conduct a face-to-face solicitation that makes everyone feel great
- The importance of planned giving
- The significance of stewardship of donors and their resources
- The value of renewing and increasing support while deepening the commitment of members (and ensuring the continued survival of the congregation)

Successful
Synagogue
Fundraising Today
Overcoming the Fear
of Asking for Money

Rabbi David A. Mersky and Abigail Harmon

For People of All Faiths, All Backgrounds

JEWISH LIGHTS Publishing

Woodstock, Vermont

Successful Synagogue Fundraising Today:
Overcoming the Fear of Asking for Money

2016 Quality Paperback Edition, First Printing
© 2016 by David A. Mersky

Library of Congress Cataloging-in-Publication Data

Names: Mersky, David A., author. | Harmon, Abigail, author.

Title: Successful synagogue fundraising today : overcoming the fear of asking for money / Rabbi David A. Mersky and Abigail Harmon.

Description: Woodstock, VT : Jewish Lights Publishing, [2016] | Includes bibliographical references.

Identifiers: LCCN 2016001766| ISBN 9781580238564 (pbk.) | ISBN 9781580238632 (ebook)

Subjects: LCSH: Synagogue fund raising. | Synagogues—United States.

Classification: LCC BM653.3 .M47 2016 | DDC 296.6/5—dc23 LC record available at http://lccn.loc.gov/2016001766

10 9 8 7 6 5 4 3 2 1

Manufactured in the United States of America
Cover art and cover and interior design: Tim Holtz

For People of All Faiths, All Backgrounds
Jewish Lights Publishing
A Division of LongHill Partners, Inc.
Sunset Farm Offices, Route 4, P.O. Box 237
Woodstock, VT 05091
Tel: (802) 457-4000 Fax: (802) 457-4004
www.jewishlights.com

Contents

Introduction

Fundraising and Development in a Twenty-First-Century Synagogue

We are living in a different world than we were generations ago. Support of a synagogue is no longer automatic or given by default. Congregations in all movements are being forced to consider their revenue streams with twenty-first-century factors in mind. Can the current dues models survive? Is the Yom Kippur appeal a more or less effective method of asking for support than in years past? Can we get the new families in our congregation excited enough to support our next initiative?

These are all valid questions, but the answers are not simple. They require us to examine the reasons behind the changes in where we give our time and money. And they necessitate an in-depth look at how we can engage and encourage a commitment to the synagogue for years to come.

A Bit of History

In the post–World War II era—when American suburbs exploded and the Jewish community developed congregations far from their prewar urban ghettos, synagogues were supported in the main by the payment of dues and building fund fees. When David (co-author of this book) was a member of the staff of the then–Union of American Hebrew Congregations, a fiscally healthy congregation received no less than 85 percent of its annual operating revenue from billable, renewable sources—dues and fees that their members paid for the privilege of affiliation. The balance of the operating budget would be covered by income from the rental of facilities, operating surpluses from preschools—often simply tenants of the congregation's building—and a fundraising event or two to celebrate achievements and balance the budget. Few congregations in the early seventies had endowments.

In recent years, congregations have experimented with various dues models from fair share—often based on a suggested percentage of a family's adjusted gross income—to "gifts from the heart"—entirely voluntary, unguided amounts. But regardless of the method of assessment and collection, membership was usually something that was billed to each head of household on the first day of the fiscal year. Member units were in fact no more than accounts receivable and never valued donors who required development or cultivation, or deserved stewardship.

Congregations can no longer depend on the dues and fees that their members pay to carry the load. Most congregations today may receive as little as 50 percent of their operating expenses by directly billing their members. In fact, many congregations today are struggling to attract members altogether, as patterns of affiliation have changed markedly. As religious a nation as the United States is, today the fastest-growing segment, according to a recent Pew study, are the "nones"—those who declare no religious affiliation or identification. (This is a subject for another book altogether.)

In this context, the question is how best to fund the twenty-first century synagogue. Our answer is through a comprehensive plan of development and fundraising.

Over the years, we both have worked as staff, volunteers, and consultants, much of the time within synagogues and organizations with strong Jewish values. We have more than sixty years combined experience in development and fundraising. We believe at our core that the synagogue is a key gateway to Jewish life, a central organizing principal of the Jewish community, and the place where, together with their families, Jews of all ages learn the value of *tzedakah*. All other Jewish communal agencies depend upon the synagogue to develop leaders with a commitment to and understanding of Jewish life.

This book is our insight into a world that is at times insular. Many adult Jews only join one synagogue—and often that is the congregation in which they were raised. They have little or no basis for comparison as to how other synagogues function or might have evolved in the twenty-first century.

While we have taken some ideas from other nonprofits, most of the fundraising and development issues about which we write are based upon the nearly quarter century of work that we have done with synagogues. This book will guide you toward current best practices within the synagogue setting and help you enhance your community by giving everyone a way to invest in the future of the Jewish people.

A Culture of Giving

You may have read about innovative alternatives to required dues systems as more congregations experiment with voluntary support systems. Some congregations, it should be noted, were founded on this latter basis. Others have turned to it in recent years. Regardless, all congregations can learn how to engage people who associate with their synagogues and consider themselves in some way as stakeholders—both personally and financially.

The good news is that philanthropy in general and support of religious entities in particular are growing enterprises. Despite the Great Recession of 2008 and 2009, when even philanthropy dipped for the first time since such records began to be maintained, giving—at least in the United States—has experienced its biggest rebound in more than four decades. According to Giving USA, which reports on philanthropy in the United States, in 2014 (the last full year for which we have data) it's estimated that Americans gave $358.4 billion.[*] The report also stated that

- Incomes are rising.
- Foundations are becoming even more generous.
- The wealthy are giving big.
- Individual people are giving more and religious giving is still strong.

Giving by individuals—living and dead—represents 80 percent of all giving. If you include giving done by family foundations that are not professionally staffed, then that number likely increases to 90 percent. Religion continues to receive the biggest share of donations—32 percent. Nearly $115 billion of the total amount contributed to all causes goes to religious enterprises. Donors who identify as religious tend to give more money than those who do not.[†] In other words, there is

---

[*] Melanie A. McKitrick, "Giving USA 2015 Annual Report on Philanthropy for 2014," Lilly Family School of Philanthropy, Indiana University, Indianapolis, IN, 2015.
[†] Ibid., p. 129.

exceptionally fertile ground among the members of your congregation for voluntary support.

Now all you need to do is understand how to leverage this strong philanthropic impulse to create an environment in which you know how and when to ask, and your members understand why they should give to your congregation beyond their dues.

Development versus Fundraising

We often hear, "We have no culture of giving." That is not true. In all likelihood, you and your members are very generous people and give to support many causes. What you really lack is a culture of asking.

To be fair, it is more than simply asking. To raise enough funds to sustain the congregation and the community who depend on it, it is key to understand the difference between development and fundraising.

In fundraising, you are figuring out how to raise money. Seeking additional funds often translates into developing new tactics. (Should you consider a gala or a raffle in addition to the Yom Kippur appeal?)

Development in the nonprofit setting is the process that manages relationships between and among stakeholders and the organization. Fundraising is a part of development, but a successful development program—essential for the fundraising results that you are looking to achieve—manages *relationships* so that donors feel valued, not taken for granted or treated as accounts receivable.

When you have read this book and used the templates and forms, your community and their commitment to the congregation will be stronger. And in that way, you will play a role in ensuring the future of Jewish life in your community.

PART I

What Can Fundraising Help You Achieve?

Chapter 1

Financial Sustainability

Increasing the Money Raised on an Annual Basis

If you have picked up this book, you are interested in improving your synagogue's fundraising. And while fundraising can help create community, identify leadership, and strengthen management systems, a successful fundraising program will also increase the money raised on an annual basis. At almost every institution around the country, there is money left unasked for and, as a result, not given.

"Wait," you might say. "We have an annual appeal every year! Every family in our congregation is asked for a donation at High Holiday services. If they haven't given, they just don't want to give to us." That may be how you perceive the interaction, but do your congregants see it the same way?

The Appeal versus the Annual Fund

Often, an annual appeal is confused with an annual fund. The roots of this misconception are obvious; the traditions of a Yom Kippur "ask," combined with cards with fold-down tabs to be handed to an usher, worked for years. And when it stopped covering the expenses, congregations relied on a few major donors to cover the shortfall (either through a personal ask or through a fundraising event), dipped into reserve funds, or simply went into the red with no decisive plan in place. The annual appeal, for all intents and purposes, was the annual fund.

But times have changed, and synagogues have to change with them.

An appeal is a onetime (or one-time-of-year) request for support. The Yom Kippur appeal serves as a reminder that synagogues need support and congregants need synagogues for the High Holidays (if not more). What better time than the peak of attendance to ask for donations?

But what if you are a family of five with three children in the school system? Assuming the children are in public school (day school or private school only exacerbates the problem), by the early fall, when the High Holidays come around, the family has often paid for school supplies, miscellaneous school fees, PTC/PTA dues, soccer fees and new cleats, music lessons and instruments, art classes and supplies, and innumerable other expenses that can range from a few dollars to thousands.

They feel as if everyone is asking for something at this time of year, and then it's the synagogue. They say to themselves, "Aren't we already paying dues and religious school fees? And now they want more?" They have donor fatigue before they have even heard the pitch.

So what can you do to change this? Well, you can ask them to cover their ears if they don't want to listen. Or, turn the annual appeal into an annual fund by considering each family as an individual ask or as a "campaign of one," an ask that is based on donor preferences, not on when the congregation needs money or thinks members should give. (This will be an important theme throughout this book).

You can and still should do the High Holiday ask, acknowledging your appreciation for past support and making the case as to why people should give, give again, or give more. But consider how to round out the year of development efforts. Consider when preschool parents would be willing to listen to the needs of the congregation (hint: it's not when they are thinking about the needs of their children transitioning to new classes) or what would really attract a couple in their late fifties (who lately have only come to services two or three times a year) to support this congregation year-round. It is not going to be the same invitation to give and it is not going to highlight the same aspects of the synagogue. And while some invitations will be face-to-face conversations, many more will be generalized but targeted to a particular stage of life and level of involvement with the congregation. If you consider what each family unit will respond to, they will feel the difference. And give differently.

To have an annual fund you will need to know:

- What aspects of the congregation a family likes to experience
- How much they gave last year
- Whether they have given in previous years, but not last year*
- What time of year they gave (not always the same as when you asked)
- What you will ask them to give this year
- How to follow up to ensure a gift

An annual fund has a development plan in place, a yearly calendar of stewardship and "moves management" activity (you will learn about moves management in chapter 15), and an understanding of who will complete each task. This is no small undertaking, but improving your fundraising will be a group effort. Let's restate that for emphasis: This is not a task for one person to do on his own and it will take effort from a team invested in a better financial outcome. Are you ready to make a change?

How Do You Define Success?

Defining success is not universal among people or even countries—so it is not surprising that a group of congregants would lack consensus. All too often, synagogue staff and leadership spend their time treading water or putting out fires. Did the mailing go out on time? Did the board members make their calls to thank this month's donors? Did the rabbi follow up with the major donor who just had a personal crisis? When we look up, we realize that weeks or months have passed. We are left feeling defeated by the massive workload that still lies ahead and lack any sense of the big picture.

What would constitute success? Or, more specifically, what is your definition of success, as a staff member, a volunteer, or a community? It's time to create your own definition(s) so that you will know when you have achieved it.

Prioritizing

For most synagogues, there is a never-ending list of changes, updates, and improvements that should be made to the building, the staff, the

---

* We often refer to lapsed donors as LYBUNTs, PYBUNTs, and/or SYBUNTs, which are acronyms for Last/Previous/Past Year/Sometime But Unfortunately Not This Year (the Y is silent).

mission, the fundraising program, the finances, the structure, and the like. Ideally, you would prioritize your resources to accomplish your goals. But the reality is that, for most people, the choice from the long to-do list is somewhat random. Maybe it is the next item on your list or the one that will affect the most people. But with the to-do list of what we could do on one side of a page, we all too often forget to look at the flip side of the page—the accomplishments. No matter how much more remains to be accomplished in the overall plan, you need to stop and feel good about what has already been done.

So stop defining success as having achieved *all* your goals (utterly impossible) and start defining your success by what you have deemed important and then accomplished (empowering).

Defining What Is Important

Say you are a list maker and there are eight tasks that you want to check off for this month. You are saying those are the eight most important parts of your job in the next month and you would consider yourself successful if you completed them (for example, make one extra stewardship move a day, engage with one potential new board member, or revisit the prospect research to consider who should be engaged in a more meaningful way). After defining the tasks, reorder your list with the first item as the most important.

If you are not a list maker, consider how you plan out your week. What do you use to remind yourself of what to do next? It is essential to define a successful week/month/year, and then to accept that, in all likelihood, you might not accomplish any major tasks that are not a component of your definition of success.

Dealing with the Unexpected

People often say that they spend so much time with the unplanned parts of their jobs—the donors who stop by and want to chat, the emergencies that arise, or the colleague who desperately needs their help—that they are constantly falling behind on what they hoped to achieve. Are you nodding your head in agreement?

Then acknowledge that as a part of your reality. Look at your work-week for the last few weeks, months, or years and consider the average time that you dedicated to these "extra" efforts. Then allot a certain percentage of your upcoming week to these tasks. Consider whether the needs change with the calendar or are steady all year round. And whether you are the right person to be helping in these situations.

Simply staying afloat cannot provide you with any measure of success beyond the knowledge that you didn't drown. But feeling successful can be the difference between satisfaction and frustration. Make sure you are making conscious decisions about your success—in development and in life.

Establishing Systems That Survive Turnover

Systems are not sexy. However, they are the structures that will accentuate your more attractive parts. Systems are the way that your donors know you take fundraising seriously and the way that your congregation creates an impression of being organized and intentional. In other words, orderly systems show that you are a good investment for a donor.

What fundraising systems are necessary for a small to midsize synagogue? For one thing, you will require fundraising software that offers:

- Prospect research
- The capability to manage contacts, their relationships to other contacts, and giving history, including:
  - Amount given
  - Time of year donations were made
  - How each donor gave (online, via email, with an unsolicited check)
  - Whether it was in response to a certain letter, email, call, or meeting
  - Whether it was in response to a life-cycle event
  - How many donations each made per year
  - Rating for a major gift
- Relationship tracking
  - Who did this donor meet with?
  - What is the next step?
  - Are any follow-up materials necessary?
  - Who will be the relationship manager for this person, going forward?

- Event and program management
  - What events or programs does the donor attend?
  - Does she volunteer for an event?
  - Does she donate items or in-kind services to a program?
- Service and training
- Pledge invoicing
- Reporting
  - By source
  - By date of most recent gift
  - By dollar range of most recent gift
  - By relationship manager
- Access for more than one person (this can be accomplished through a cloud-based system or a multiuser agreement)

Access to software for more than one person is often ignored in small synagogues. People think there will only ever be one person entering the information at a time or you only have one person on your development team so one user should be enough. But housing your data on one person's laptop or giving full control to only one person is taking a huge gamble. Laptops get lost. Files get damaged. People change jobs and forget to transfer all the information.

Often, if fundraising is not an organizational priority, software doesn't get updated on a regular basis. That leads to a system so clunky that only one person knows how to access the data or it is too hard to use and the person in charge ends up supplementing with Excel spreadsheets or Word documents that are created to solve a specific problem. Of course, that causes a whole host of other issues. Who has the latest version of the annual appeal spreadsheet? Did everyone receive and open the email with the latest version of the member donations for the gala? Is the information tagged so that you can find who attended the spring preschool fundraiser?

New software packages enable you to do more online than before, which allows for flexibility, automatic software updates, and a higher retention of data. This, in turn, leads to easier data entry, higher-quality data, and faster access to the information. And much of it is geared toward small to midsize synagogues. Then you can focus on the quality of events, donor satisfaction, and donor retention.

Planning for a Capital Campaign

Smart congregations get their annual fund and fundraising in shape before they initiate a capital campaign. Creating new methods and systems is much easier when you are not on a clock to "go public" with a $12 million campaign. So how will you know if you are ready for a capital campaign?

Your Community

Do you have the full support of your community of stakeholders? If you have been stewarding donors and practicing moves management, you will already know who your largest donors will likely be, who would be most likely to serve on the fundraising committee for a campaign, and whether or not they think you need a new building/wing/sanctuary/religious school/preschool/endowment. You need to have a finger on the pulse of the community. And an understanding as to whether they will they give their financial support.

In addition, do you have a corps of people who are willing to do the work to raise the millions of dollars that will be required? You need administrators, solicitors, and marketers who understand what it will take to fulfill the promises you make when you start the campaign and continue until you finish and exceed your goal. You need bankers, attorneys, and accountants. You need a diverse committee that will help fulfill your vision.

Infrastructure

Consider the following:

- Who will create the structure for the campaign?
- Who will keep track of prospect assignments, meetings, results, and all the required documentation?
- Who will set benchmarks and deadlines, and check in periodically to make sure you are achieving the interim results as planned?
- Will you do it all in-house or hire a development consultant?

Nonprofits can do a capital campaign on their own, but they should understand the steps and have a clear plan before they start the process. You'll need to keep everyone motivated to keep moving forward—even when the campaign stalls or feels as if it has been going on forever.

Timing

What factors will affect your timing? Consider the length of your quiet phase and what benchmarks need to be reached before you go public. This will be affected by:

- Staff capacity
- Finding a campaign chair and leadership
- Establishing a fundraising capital campaign committee without decimating the synagogue's current fundraising committee and its efficacy
- Where the High Holidays fall during the time frame (Will you be able to hold services during construction, if construction is part of your development plan?)
- Summer schedules

Capital campaigns show the true nature of your congregation. Are you the kind of community in which it is worth investing millions of dollars or are you struggling to even get your thank-you letters out each month? The impression that you give from the very beginning of the process will make the difference between success and failure. Outside development consultants help in a variety of ways, such as focusing energy on important tasks, increasing success rates through improved systems, and training solicitors. Yet no one can help a congregation that does not have the community support, necessary infrastructure, and understanding of timing and timeliness.

Chapter 2

Building Community

An Added Benefit of Successful Fundraising

Does Your Community Support Your Mission and Your Vision?

All nonprofits—whether they are religious institutions or not—understand that they need mission and vision statements. The truth is, many mission and vision statements for reform congregations could be interchangeable. The same could be said for other movements, as well as unaffiliated congregations. But that does not make these declarations any less impactful. There is something unifying about congregations across the country having similar missions.

That being said, mission and vision statements do have to stay current and relevant to the needs of an individual congregation in order to continue to garner support from that community.

When is it time to consider whether you need a new mission or vision statement?

- You are about to start a strategic planning process.
- You have had a major change in staff or board leadership.
- You are establishing or revamping an annual fund.
- You are considering a capital campaign.
- You want to provide the congregation with a shared focus.
- You have founders' syndrome (the founders are still active and restricting growth or change).
- You are about to work with a consultant for a feasibility study.

- Your mission or vision statement was created before the turn of the twenty-first century. (Consider the changes that have happened in the world since 1999, like the fact that the BlackBerry used to be considered impressive technology.)

Do You Need New Mission and Vision Statements?

If the leadership feels that your current mission and vision statements still represent the congregation, skip to the next section. If not, consider the following when you are creating or updating the mission or vision statements:

- The mission and vision statements should be able to continue to represent you into the future. A strategic plan can determine the specific direction for lifelong learning, spiritual focus, worship, community activities, and building needs over the next five years. The mission and vision should be far-reaching and broader in scope.
- Keep it short. Current theories suggest that both the mission and the vision should be one sentence (albeit sometimes long sentences). That will keep the focus clear and concise.
- Avoid making a Franken-statement. This may sound familiar: Jerry thinks the concept of diversity and inclusion is essential. Rachel feels that they have to include a reference to *tikkun olam* and *chesed*. Leah insists that no statement would be complete without referring to the geographic location served. Michael wants the amazing education program for all learners to be highlighted. And Eric is just trying to write something that will please everyone. It is a recipe for a Frankenstein-like statement that informs but will not inspire anyone—even if the reasoning behind each voice is sound and the sentiment is admirable.
- There are important aspects to the congregation beyond the mission or vision statement. In other words, there are many valued aspects of a nonprofit that are not listed in a mission statement. This will not be the only sentence a prospective member or colleague will read about the organization.

- Once the committee has created the new statement(s), bring it to the board, asking for approval, not for input. If a committee has been charged with crafting these valuable representations of the congregation, the board should not have a chance to rework them. If any board members feel that they should have a voice, invite them to the next committee meeting. By the time you are asking for board approval you are inviting the board to offer impressions and highlight anything that feels unrepresentative. What to do with those impressions is up to the committee.
- Consider whether your community will support your mission and vision statements. While the board is, in theory, representative of the membership, they are often considered "insiders." Would people who feel like they are not integral to the congregation's existence agree that this represents the entire congregation? This is worth considering.

After reading the last section and deciding that your mission and/or vision statement no longer fits, ask yourself this: Does your current statement need to be tweaked or completely rewritten? Here is a list of questions designed to help you through the process. Maybe this will be the first step in your new planning process. Or the next step in knowing that your congregation is already on the right path.

Mission Statement

- Is the mission statement still current? Does it feel fresh and inspiring?
- Do the board, staff, and volunteers understand the mission and agree that is the focus of your organization? Can they explain it to someone in an elevator pitch or a more extensive conversation?
- Pull out your latest newsletter. Do the programs listed help you fulfill your mission? Is there any part of your mission that is not currently being fulfilled? If there are programs that are community supported but not part of your mission, what does that say about your mission?
- Does the wording give everyone a true understanding of the organization and its purpose? Is it too complex or too oblique?

- Is each word there to help further your mission? Take out one or more and see how that changes the impact.

Vision Statement

- Does your vision statement describe what you hope to achieve as a congregation? Is it feasible?
- When you consider a new program, do you consider whether it will help realize your vision?
- Do you feel motivated when you read it? Will others? Think of it as an easy way to share inspiration.
- How long will your vision statement last? Is this a five-year vision? Ten-year? Is it achievable or pie-in-the-sky?
- Is it specific to who will benefit from your vision? People want to know if you plan on serving the same population or additional groups, the same number of people with more focus on specific areas, or a broader range of services.
- Is your vision visionary?

Different Constituencies: From the Preschool to the Daily Minyan

Religious institutions are unique as nonprofits because they work to serve members at each and every stage of life. It is much easier to focus on providing meals to the elderly or inspiring urban teenagers to engage in dance. Well, it's easier in that the target audience is easier to find.

Temples, churches, and mosques (among others) are, in some ways, trying to be all things to all people. This is a monumental task for limited staff and volunteer leadership to take on. Let's start by examining the demographics in an average midsize synagogue.

- *Preschool families.* Whether or not you have a preschool, there needs to be enough activity to draw in this crowd on a regular basis and allow parents to engage with similar families. This is often a feeder source for the religious school and for general membership.
- *The K–7, pre–b'nai mitzvah children and their families.* This is the peak of membership for many Jewish families. They may be easy to get in the door, but how do you engage them beyond religious school classes so that children and their parents want to stay involved after their b'nai mitzvah?

- *Post–b'nai mitzvah children and precollege teenagers.* Youth groups, Hebrew High, and Confirmation classes can offer this crowd something interesting and fun—so their association with Judaism and a synagogue is more than classroom time.
- *The college and postcollege set (eighteen- to twenty-six-year-olds).* They are still looking for a connection to a place where they have felt comfortable, but they're not quite ready to join a congregation on their own. Oftentimes, they are not yet in a serious romantic relationship and they're looking for strong connections and roots in an uncertain time. They may be either off at college or living in another area, not necessarily the place where they grew up.
- *Young couples prechildren.* They have made a home together, but should they become members of a congregation? Why should they join yours? If their peers are involved, the answer is obvious.
- *Singles.* Whether by choice or for lack of the right partner, many people stay single later into life or their entire lives. Depending on the community, this can be a large number or small, but either way, they have the time to be involved, if they're given a reason to.
- *Couples with no children.* Not everyone wants children or wants to feel that the only attraction for members involves children. They will be joined by members who want adult learning in a child-free environment—especially as the children get older and need less focused parental involvement. Should these couples take a class at the congregation or at the museum down the road? It all depends on the offerings.
- *Empty nesters.* Now that their children are gone, is there something to attract them beyond the services? Are their friends still involved? Are they taking leadership roles now that they have the time?
- *Retirees.* People retire at different ages these days, but in this case we will focus on the seventy-five-plus crowd. They often summer or winter in a different community. Is there enough to engage them when they are in your town? As they pass eighty, they may go to assisted living communities or need more support from the community. In addition to the flavor retirees add, they have more time to attend lectures and events, if they are timed appropriately.

Those are demographic descriptions. But what inspires passion in your community? These groups may include:

- The daily minyan
- The chorus
- *Chesed* volunteers
- Lecture attendees
- Social activists
- Supporters of Israel
- Regular worship participants
- People involved in life-cycle events
- Arts and creative opportunity types
- Brotherhood and Sisterhood members

Each congregation is unique and should add its own list of groups that seek and find engagement. The key takeaway should be that you are conscious of how members interact and experience life within your walls and within your community.

Finding Your Volunteer Leadership

A strong nonprofit has a pipeline of past, present, and future leadership, and congregations should not be an exception. But what if you have not been as diligent as you should have been over the past five or ten years? It's not too late to catch up, but it is time to make it a high priority.

Step 1: Establish a Governance and Leadership Committee

Examining your current board and seeking new volunteer leadership requires a standing committee that will work on a continual basis on this essential task.

What will this committee do?

- Assess the current makeup of your board.
- Propose criteria for and select prospective board members.
- Cultivate a confidential, cumulative, ongoing list of prospective board members.
- Recruit prospective candidates.
- Present candidates to the board for approval.

- Orient new members to their responsibilities.
- Involve members in the life and work of the board.
- Recognize and celebrate their achievements as a board.
- Plan for each individual board member's self-assessment and an annual board evaluation.
- Create opportunities for personal development through retreats and education at each board meeting.

Step 2: Assess the Current Make-up of Your Board

Understanding your current board—demographics, skills, strengths, skill gaps, length of tenure, and giving history—will help you know the types of people you need.

Step 3: Cultivate a Confidential, Cumulative, Ongoing List of Prospective Board Members

Presumably, each year you gather a list of prospective board members and determine who should be invited to join. Ideally, this happens in a governance and leadership development committee, but sometimes it happens in an ad hoc nominating committee or the executive committee.

What happens to those names and that information after the meeting? Is that information retained for future meetings in an organized and logical way? Or is the institutional knowledge that Sarah Goldman wants to be on the board but she is currently the middle school PTC president lost? If not recorded, all that is remembered is that Sarah Goldman said no, when what she meant was not now. And then she wonders why she is never approached again.

Strong boards plan for succession. One of the most important responsibilities a board member undertakes is to replace himself with an even better board member. That ensures the congregation will thrive for years to come.

Changing the Synagogue Culture from a Membership Mentality to a Donor-Centered Nonprofit Mentality

For generations, Jewish life was experienced through congregational memberships and community center participation. In post–World War II America, membership in a church or synagogue was expected—an

American value and obligation. Many Jews with any semblance of religious identity—or, at least, a need to educate their children and celebrate the rite of passage of a bar or bat mitzvah—were members of a synagogue. Such affiliation was a symbol of support for Judaism, Israel, and their community.

Now participation is optional. And the reason? In part, because it is viewed as membership.

Those same members who view every nickel and dime they give to their congregation as a fee-for-service give money to nonprofits who offer them good feelings in return. They complain about a $15 fee for a program at the synagogue, but they are willing to pay $20 to go to the movies or $100 to go to a concert or a ball game. While that may seem unfair, the flip side is that it presents an opportunity for each and every congregation to engage members as donors and encourage additional financial contributions.

The Membership Mentality

Today, "membership mentality" is the idea that belonging to a congregation is transaction-based. You pay for dues to get access to services, High Holiday tickets, religious school, bar or bat mitzvah dates, classes, and pastoral care, when needed. With the exception of pastoral care, many of those services come with additional fees. "So," they think, "what are the membership dues for? And why don't they cover all the expenses?"

The bills come in every year or every month and, each time, your members consider how little they utilize the congregation's offerings. It's akin to seeing the gym membership show up on your credit card bill, knowing that you haven't been there in months. It feels like a waste of money even if you want to go more often. Should you cancel the membership or pledge to show up more?

Donor-Centered Mentality

What if we could step into a time machine and go back to a time when dues were the support of the Jewish community—for you, your family, your friends, and for others who were less fortunate? The good news is it's possible to regain that culture of supporting the Jewish community. The bad news is that the membership mentality has to be uprooted—from the congregants up to the staff and volunteer leadership.

While dues—whether based on traditional models or a more flexible version—may still be required, this will mean shifting your focus to your annual fund. And annual fund donations are *contributions* and should be treated as such.

Nonprofits have to treat each donation as a gift—not an expectation. An $18 donation to the rabbi's discretionary fund is acknowledged by a form letter. A $25 donation to a family services agency gets the person on a list of donors to be stewarded and researched to determine if they might, at one time, become a major donor. More work? Yes. Better results? Definitely. That onetime gift may be in honor of a *simcha*, but it shows that the donor is willing and able to give more than the dues.

A little change in perspective goes a long way. Members are billed, but donors are engaged as if they have the potential and the inclination to give more.

The Congregation as a Nonprofit

Something else to consider is how your members view the synagogue. While everyone knows religious institutions are nonprofits, if finances and donations were not discussed in their childhood home, many people have no idea if their parents paid dues or were charitable to their synagogue. Among the questions people often ask are these: "Is everyone supposed to donate for a *yahrzeit*, even if they won't be at services?" "Why would I give to a discretionary fund?" "How much would I give to thank my congregation's rabbi for officiating at a baby-naming?" "I see the lists of who gave, but how do I know when it is appropriate to give?"

There is a level of knowledge that is assumed in many congregations that is not assumed in a nonprofit organization. It's as if being born into Judaism is enough to understand the inner workings of a synagogue, or the expectation that by being a member for twenty years, you know how a memorial fund or discretionary fund is used. Some people would never think to proactively search for a greater understanding of these concepts. But does that mean they wouldn't want to support the congregation in these ways?

Instead of alienating prospective donors, engage *everyone* as a prospective donor and help them feel that they are making a difference with each gift, no matter how large or small.

Consider the difference between these two approaches:

1. Please give to our Yom Kippur appeal.
2. The annual appeal is our congregation-wide development effort. Many revenue sources—in addition to congregational membership dues—support our warm and inclusive synagogue committed to learning, justice, and good deeds. We are proud of our inspiring worship services and programs—offered twelve months a year—for members and neighbors. A few highlights include:

   - Over six hundred students in our religious school. They participate through our acclaimed distance-learning program for elementary-school-aged learners and Beit Midrash, an elective program for middle school and high school students.
   - The Purim Carnival and Mitzvah Day.
   - Collaborations with a plethora of Jewish communal agencies and organizations such as Hebrew Union College–Jewish Institute of Religion, American Israel Public Affairs Committee (AIPAC), American Jewish World Service (AJWS), the Jewish Community Center, the Shalom Hartman Institute, and the Lehrhaus for Lifelong Learning.

   Heartfelt thanks to everyone who has contributed to this year's annual appeal! Participation from each and every congregant is a sign of the amazing and caring community that is Congregation Emanuel, and enables us to achieve the vision we share for our community.

For additional examples of online pages that can be used in offline copy that really encourages donations, visit the following sites' donation pages (and note how easy it is to find the donation pages):

- Oxfam.org
- New York Public Library (www.nypl.org)
- San Diego Zoo (http://zoo.sandiegozoo.org)
- Temple Beth Shalom of Needham, Massachusetts (https://tbsneedham.org)*

---

*Full disclosure: Abigail is a member and donor here.

What do other nonprofits offer to donors at certain levels?

- Naming opportunities
- Special access to events
- Advance tickets to events
- Private stewardship events
- House parties to get to know other members

There is something to be said for creating a synagogue for the entire community and not just for the wealthy, but there should be a balance. No one is surprised when a major donor is asked to host a gala at a synagogue or any other nonprofit. Why should it be surprising that a donor would get access to a private dinner with a resident scholar? Or advance tickets to a special event? Everyone is welcome to experience the scholar's teachings and attend the event, but we live in a world in which VIP treatment is accorded those who make major donations. And while that might not be the reason they give, it might be the reason they continue to give or upgrade to a higher giving level.

Of course, the priority is to keep access to the congregation's offerings open to all. But to have exciting lectures and special musicians requires funding above and beyond the membership dues. Treating your synagogue's donors like valued funders will increase your revenue while improving the community for all.

Chapter 3

The Major Gift Engagement Plan

The real job of development—which is not just a euphemism for fundraising—is to "develop" and nurture relationships through a disciplined process of follow-up and involvement that ultimately leads to a face-to-face solicitation. The annual fund is the foundation of every great development program. It provides an opportunity to identify, interest, involve, engage, and acknowledge generous donors. A thoughtful approach to creating a development plan—communication and contact, moves management, solicitation, and stewardship—creates lifelong donors.

Why Create a Formalized Plan?

The fear of not achieving your fundraising goals is rooted in the absence of a plan, when you cannot see a path forward.

It is easy to talk about identifying or acknowledging major donors, but doing the work requires a formalized plan that includes a strategy, calendar, tactics, benchmarks, and end goals.

Then you need to determine who will be involved, who will be responsible for each task, and who will be leading the charge. Volunteer leadership is crucial, but so is a dedicated staff member who will act as the point person.

A plan clarifies that you are looking toward the future of the synagogue and all it can be. What will you need? Where will you have potential staff turnover? Is there a need for someone on staff with different skills to execute your plan? Is that person junior or senior to your current staff?

While it is scary to move ahead with an ambitious plan, an organization that is not financially secure and appears to only be treading water does not look like a good philanthropic investment. Above all, improving your fundraising capacity will require you to prove that you are a good investment.

Major Gift Engagement Plan

The focus on major gifts is rooted in Pareto's Principle (first identified by nineteenth-century Italian economist Vilfredo Pareto), known as the 80/20 rule. That means that 80 percent of your revenue will come from 20 percent of your donors. In this generation, it has probably moved closer to 90/10.

The following chart offers you the opportunity to examine the steps you will need to engage major gift prospects and donors (however you define them), your internal deadlines for completion, who will be responsible for each aspect of the plan, and a level of accountability to assess whether you are making progress. This overview will be explained in detail throughout this book.

Executing the Plan

Once you have created a solid plan that includes segmenting your membership, researching prospects, and planning a series of moves for each person or couple, it is time to execute. Here is a list of ways to improve your chances for success:

1. Focus on no more than one or two specific goals, for example:
   * Number of gifts that will be increased by 10 percent
   * Number of new gifts of $1,000+
   * Amount of money in gifts of $5,000+ as compared to last year
   * Increase 50 percent of all donors to $1,000 donors
2. Act on lead measures (see below) and keep a compelling scoreboard.
   * Differentiate between lag measures (Have you achieved the goal?) and lead measures—activities that influence whether you are likely to achieve the goal.

The Major Gift Engagement Plan

Step	Target Date	Who Is Responsible?	Achieved?
Segment your existing donor database and select your best major gift prospects, ranking them from A to D (see p. 106 for an explanation).			
Starting with those in the "A" category, create a "file" for each.			
Collect easy-to-access research.			
Consider whether there is enough data or whether you should pay for prospect research.			
Identify and consult with natural partners for the top twenty prospects; natural partners are volunteers who can help in the development of the relationship with each prospect.			
Develop a strategy and gift objectives for each prospect.			
Plan five to ten "moves" for each prospect—a series of steps, such as emails, letters, newsletters, phone calls, events, or one-on-one encounters that will "move" these prospects toward their next (or first) gift.			
Continue to update the file(s) to note what you have learned through each move and follow-up call.			
Create an individualized plan, sometimes called a "campaign of one," for each prospect.			
Modify the plan(s) as needed—these are not static, but dynamic—as circumstances and new information warrant.			
Identify and consult with natural partners for the next twenty prospects.			
Repeat steps from above for each prospective donor.			

- If the goal is to increase major gifts revenue from $X to $Y, here are examples of lead measures that would appear on the scoreboard:
  - Each member of the development team will complete four face-to-face visits per week with legitimate prospects.
  - Ask for something on each visit—this can be for advice on something specific, additional funds, or work toward a volunteer effort. Asking is a way to encourage interest and engagement.
  - Document the quality and results of each visit.
  - Follow up within forty-eight hours after each visit to get feedback from the prospect, provide any information requested, and develop next steps, including when you will speak again.
3. Create a cadence of accountability through a weekly meeting so that:
   - Each volunteer or staff member can report on prior commitments made at last week's meeting, such as "I will conduct five visits."
   - Review the scoreboard and learn from successes and failures.
   - Plan for the coming week and make new commitments of activity.
4. Celebrate achieving your weekly goals.
   - With each renewed, upgraded, or even new gift, celebrate by informing your colleagues, your leadership, and most especially your donors. The easiest way to do this is through your regularly scheduled newsletter, but "shout-outs" about a particularly meaningful gift will help build excitement and keep momentum going.
   - Help solicitors keep track of accomplishments throughout the year; that way, they will become even more invested and involved. And it feels good to see your own work in the aggregate.
5. Steward every relationship faithfully. That's the only way to ensure that you will never again fall short or have to scramble for new donors.

Evaluating Your Process

If there is no method to monitor success, can you be successful?

If you created a development plan, then goals and time lines were put in place. Now you need to contemplate whether the plan is achieving your goals or falling short, exciting volunteers or exhausting them, creating new relationships or destroying connections.

Ideally the plan is moving smoothly and you can set up a quarterly meeting for your committee that will include a check-in, highlight achievements, and note any areas that have to be improved. However, if the process feels like it is at a standstill, it is time to set up more frequent meetings focused on the process, maybe even weekly. Acknowledge whether there are any flaws are in the plan, the systems, or the people.

Accountability helps you achieve your congregation's goals. Creating a plan is important, as is understanding your donors. But doing what you say you are going to do as a volunteer is the difference between financial security and a lot of wasted time for everyone involved. Make this clear from the start to each person charged with working toward your new goals.

Aside from accountability, what, specifically, makes for successful regular meetings? Factors that can affect the process include:

- How often your committee meets.
- The day of the week or time of day that will help you achieve critical mass.
- Changing the staff point person.
- Record-keeping methods. Are your records kept on a Google spreadsheet, an Excel document, or direct access to fundraising software? Who "owns" the information?
- Whether the record keeper is collecting the data in a way that works for the volunteers *and* the record keeper. When, how often, and by what means should updates be sent?
- Data entry methods. Is everything going into the database on a regular basis? Have there been missing or duplicate records? What went wrong and how can it be prevented in the future?
- Follow-up steps that are easy to achieve and are being done on a regular basis. Telling a donor you will follow up and then not doing what you said may seem minor, but it can set you back

months, if not years, in credibility and your rating as a worthy philanthropic investment.

Staffing and leadership concerns include:

- Is the staff person the right person to do the job? Does she have the time to focus on promoting this process? Does she need additional training?
- Is the chair of the committee leading the way? Has he made his own gift? Has he been accountable to staff, fellow volunteers, and donors? Is he helping the process or merely lending his name?
- Do you have enough volunteers on board? Are the volunteers accountable to staff, fellow volunteers, and donors? Are your volunteers willing and able to make an ask for a specific dollar amount? Do you need to pair up volunteers willing to do the legwork with people willing to make the financial ask? Are the volunteers giving timely updates to the record keeper?

Assume Ramp-up Time as You Initiate Your Systems

Your first development plan incorporating new ways to engage donors may take a bit more time to carry out than expected. That does not mean failure. But it does mean that the plan should take less time for execution the following year. There is a learning curve that should be expected—by both you and the donor—if you are determined to make major changes to improve your congregational life.

It Seems to Be Going Well. Now What?

Once a development program is running smoothly, you should be considering what new and fresh ideas could enhance it. How could you reduce costs? What needs are not being met? Could you expand the number of people being cultivated? Could you come up with some new ways to encourage more volunteers to join the cause? Could you increase your current goal by 25 percent over three years? If so, how? The possibilities are endless if you continue to challenge yourselves to achieve more.

PART II

Who Should Be Charged with Fundraising?

Chapter 4

Volunteer Leaders

Development Committee: An Overview

Every congregation should have a standing development committee. The development committee is charged with planning and implementing the congregation's overall development program—including fundraising. The committee members work alongside the clergy and professional staff. The development committee is staffed by the congregation's professional fundraising staff, who retain the records and ensure accountability.

The development committee focuses the congregation and its board on essential elements in the fundraising process. This includes constant attention to the following:

- The current strength of the mission and the case for supporting the congregation.
- Ways in which the congregation makes itself transparent and accountable to its stakeholders through regular communication.
- The involvement of individuals and segments of the membership with the entire congregation.
- The resources required to carry out the mission.
- Preparation of plans for soliciting the funds needed to carry out the mission.
- Assistance in the raising of funds.
- Stewardship of the funds received and the donors who gave them.

The development committee manages the board's participation in development and fundraising, as well as creating and overseeing the implementation of the congregation's development plans. Remember, the development committee should not have to do all the board's fund-raising; all board members share this crucial responsibility.

Finding Committed Volunteers

Finding development committee volunteers is a lot like finding donors. You start with the low-hanging fruit. But not everyone has the right temperament, the passion to dedicate the necessary hours, or the skill set. So how do you choose?

Fundraising Committee Questionnaire

Factors to Consider	Answer
Composition of the Committee	
How many people do you want on your development committee?	
What percentage of the committee should be board members?	
Do you want any nonboard members involved?	
Are there members of the congregation who like to do fundraising for a specific event or fund and should be invited to join the overall development committee?	
Hands-on Fundraising	
Are prospective committee members willing to research, email, phone, and meet with prospects?	
Are they willing to meet with people they do not know?	
Can they be discreet when they know someone's capacity level?	
If they have never done this before, are they willing to be trained?	
Attitude of Potential Committee Members	
Do they always have to be right?	
Do they play well with others?	
If they hear a no, will they be disheartened?	
Do they have a generally positive view of life?	
Do you want to work with these people over the next year or more?	

The Right Answers

Are there correct answers? Every synagogue is different, but there are definitely parameters that will help you determine how you can help choose a committee with the best potential to achieve your goals.

Composition of the Committee

How many people do you want on your development committee? Ideally, the development committee will have eight to ten members, with a minimum of five members. Why is five the minimum? This is a somewhat personal preference, but follow the logic. Assuming that you have a chairperson and the board president on the committee, you will need at least three other people to come up with thoughtful ideas, represent areas of the membership that want to raise money, and help raise the money.

Will five people be enough to alter the fundraising model in a substantial way? It will be hard, but it can be done, especially in a smaller congregational setting. Eight to ten members would be a better starting point. With more members, you will have the flexibility to give out assignments based on interest as opposed to making everyone feel as though they have to do everything in order to get it all done.

The maximum number of members depends on what your committee hopes to achieve and how much work you will have for each individual. If you get beyond ten, it may be hard, at first, to distribute meaningful work to everyone. Without specific assignments, members may feel as if their time is not well spent and that they are not helping to achieve the committee's goals. Or worse, your committee members may feel they are not *really* needed and shift those volunteer hours they thought they committed to you to other activities. And the shift back will not be as easy.

What percentage of the committee should be board members? While the development committee is a good way to assess a prospective board member's interest, commitment level, and work habits, the large majority of committee members should be board members. For example, if you have eight committee members, at least five should be board members. Why? Because the development committee's job is to financially support the community whose mission and vision are guided by the board. The board should know how the funds are being raised, by whom, and for what purposes. It will encourage them to work harder on fundraising, as well as appreciate the work that is done on their behalf.

Do you want any nonboard members involved? As we mentioned above, the development committee is a good place to help the board get to know potential board members, but the opposite is also true. Non-board members on the development committee will get to know how the synagogue functions, for better or worse.

In general, it is probably best to have no more than three nonboard members on the committee to minimize their overall influence. Non-board members should never have a majority stake in a committee that significantly affects every other aspect of the congregation. They also should not be privy to the personal information of members.

> *Note: It is often customary to withhold certain information from the majority of the development committee (both board and non-board members) to respect the privacy of particular people in a community. You can offer information on an as-needed basis but be respectful of those who do not want their finances to be public knowledge. We delve more deeply into confidentiality issues in chapter 8.*

Are there members of the congregation who like to do fundraising for a specific event or fund and should be invited to join the overall development committee? To ensure a cohesive fundraising effort, every dollar raised throughout the congregation has to be raised under the umbrella of the development committee. Before you say, "The Sisterhood funds only go toward Sisterhood projects" or "Parents only give to the preschool to support the programs for the two- to five-year-old set," remember that this is not about the individual programs they benefit. There has to be a balance between congregational needs and earmarked funds.

There is no doubt that preschool parents want their donations to benefit the area they use in the congregation. But by choosing a synagogue preschool, they are a part of a larger community. They may or may not choose to take advantage of toddler services or dinners in the sukkah, but these opportunities are part of what makes the preschool a warm, welcoming environment.

But, more importantly, if the Sisterhood raises money directly from Claire Newman, will they know that she also gives to the preschool PTC or that she is going through a divorce that might affect her ability to give anything for the next few years? And while understanding Claire's overall situation might not seem important to the programs that receive the funding—after all, they are making their budget—you never want to rob Peter to pay Paul. A congregation will not be a strong community, appealing to people at different stages of life and attractive to new members, if it has four programs that are well funded and an annual deficit that ties its hands in seven other programmatic areas.

Try looking at each donor and considering an overall strategy for giving to the synagogue and its programs. In the ask, you might also say: "We know that last year you gave $180 to the Sisterhood and $75 to the preschool. This year, we noticed that you will also have a child in the religious school. We were hoping you could join us in supporting the next stages of your family, as well as the community at large, with a gift of $500 to the annual fund from which we will designate $250 to the programs that you have traditionally supported."

Another reason to have representation from those who support various areas of the congregation on your development committee is to have diverse interests represented in the fundraising strategy. It helps create an overall fundraising calendar and brings additional knowledge about an individual or family that can help the committee create a donor strategy that will benefit the entire congregation.

Hands-on Fundraising

Are prospective committee members willing to research, email, phone, and meet with prospects? How many people do you have on the committee who prefer to do the prep work before the meeting? Every committee member is valuable in achieving your goals, until you have more researchers than you have people willing to meet with prospects. Contrary to what many people think, you will not raise more money for your congregation by just adding email solicitations or sending more letters. You can try to convince yourself that you can raise more money without face-to-face solicitations, but we have a combined sixty years of experience and, trust us, you cannot.

Are they willing to meet with people they do not know? The first people you solicit will be the board, followed quickly by the congregation members your committee knows well. Shortly thereafter, you will begin to meet with people whom you know only superficially—friends of friends you met at a party or see each week at shul. But there will come a time, and pretty quickly if you are expanding your prospect list, that no one on the committee will know the people who remain on the list (and the list will still be relatively long). Make sure you have committee members who are willing to do something that will feel like a cold call, but is, in reality, a very warm and welcoming call from one congregation member to another.

Can they be discreet when they know someone's capacity level? As we mentioned earlier, fundraising offers access to personal data about finances, life events, and pastoral issues that are not for public consumption. Understanding that conversations should not leave the room—and should not even be shared with a spouse—is easier for some than others. Answering this question requires honesty about a potential development committee member's willingness and ability to maintain confidentiality, as opposed to sharing information and gossip.

If they have never done this before, are they willing to be trained? Most of the time, this is an easy answer. If they have not done fundraising but are looking to join this committee, they are interested in gaining a new skill. If they are doing it because they were pressured by a friend, they may be disruptive or members of the committee in name only—which is no help to your fundraising effort, even if they are the largest donors in the synagogue.

Attitude

Do they always have to be right? When considering someone for the committee, ask yourself this: Is she the type of person who is trying to share her truth or convince you that what she is saying is the truth? There will be a lot of negotiations during a development committee meeting. For instance, should you ask the Kartens for $100,000 or $25,000? Will Leah or Jennifer be a better fundraising event chair? Is this the time to start a capital campaign? Members of your development committee need to engage in open conversation and discussions; these are much more important than any one person being right. Committee members who need to be right will not help your effort, even if, again, they are the largest donors in the synagogue.

Do they play well with others? This is another question that relates to whether the attitude of prospective committee members will help or hinder your process. And the answer to whether or not they "have to be right" holds true here, too.

If they hear a no, will they be disheartened? Fundraising feels very personal when you are asking someone for money. You have to muster the courage to prepare for the meeting and make the call to set up the appointment. You have to have a face-to-face conversation, reading nonverbal signs and considering how best to steer the conversation toward an ask. You have to ask for a meaningful gift. The prospective donor just has to decide whether he feels it is the right gift for him at this time.

You can improve your chances by making the right ask at the right time in the right way for the right amount. However, in the end, the amount donors give will not be based on you as a person. At times it will be predetermined, which makes it even less about the solicitor. Your skills may encourage the prospect to increase, reconsider, or discuss her decision more with her spouse, but the amount is not based on whether she likes you as a person. In fact, she would not have taken the meeting if she didn't like you. For the prospect, it is about the gift, not the solicitor. You can't take it personally if she says no. What you can do is work to turn it into a "not at this time," leaving the door open for future gifts.

Do they have a generally positive view of life? There was once a theory that people could be described by the various characters of Winnie the Pooh (although we have also heard something similar about Peanuts). An Eeyore who sees the world through a gloomy lens is rarely a valuable addition to a development committee. Gloominess can translate into realism, but talking about the worst-case scenarios is often depressing and casts a negative pall over the room.

Eeyore may keep expectations in check and dreams within realistic boundaries, but asking someone to contribute a meaningful gift to a project requires the optimism of a Tigger. How else will you help others join you in increasing their annual fund gifts, convince them that their gifts will make a difference, and/or that the project will move forward?

Continuing to ask, even when the goals seem too hard to reach, too scary, or too new to try, requires a strong sense of optimism.

Do you want to work with these people over the next year or more? A development committee is a working committee. It will meet quite often at times, particularly when you are looking to dramatically change the way you raise money. Do you want to see this person, chat with her before or after a meeting, and share successes and less-than-ideal outcomes with her on a regular basis? And say it with us one last time: People who do not meet this qualification will not be helpful to your effort, even if they are the largest donors in the synagogue.

Low-Hanging Fruit

First, consider your current donors as prospective development committee members. If they are already giving you money, asking for their time should be easy. Of course, many will not be able to offer you hours on end, but you don't need to ask them to start at ten hours a week. And even if they say no, they will be flattered that you see them as someone who can be valuable beyond the dollars they provide.

What if they tell you they have very limited time, but might be able to help? Assessing each individual is important. If there is someone you think would be a valuable contributor to the overall effort, but joining a standing committee would be too intimidating for him, consider short-term options or an equally creative idea that is specific to your situation. But make it a commitment. Offer up two or three time-bound volunteer opportunities (each with a specified beginning, middle, and end that may range from one day to six months or less). Try to gauge whether he would prefer mornings or evenings, direct solicitation or behind-the-scenes work. A follow-up phone call within a few days of his initial assignment is essential to know whether the experience was positive, whether it was what he expected, and whether he would be interested in volunteering again.

As an added bonus, transitioning a donor into a volunteer will forge a stronger connection between the donor and the congregation. This will translate into the deeper relationship that you are seeking and often into increased donations.

Second, take a closer look at the people who are in the building on a regular basis. Whether they attend weekly services or drop off their children at preschool, they are the people who are the most invested in the financial sustainability of your congregation. And even if they say no, the conversation will still help in the overall stewardship of these valuable members.

Still not sure you have the volunteer pool that you think you need to succeed? Cultivate volunteerism at every opportunity. Every time a person fills out a form (religious school sign-up, event check-in, adult education, and the like), include a sentence on the form that asks if she would like to volunteer and, if so, in what capacity. You can ask if she would like to volunteer at that specific event or program next year or if she would like to help at the next Sisterhood event, or offer a checklist of ways she could help in the religious school (or another congregational area).

If the volunteer opportunity you offer is too general, you will probably get fewer responses. It often feels overwhelming to volunteer for anything that comes up. However, if you do want to leave it as an open-ended invitation to volunteer, it will continually remind people that you are looking for volunteers. When you approach someone as an individual, he will already know you are looking for volunteers. And that means that yours is a synagogue seeking new involvement and not simply relying on an exclusive group.

How about social media? If you have spent time building your congregation's social media presence, that is a great way to ask for volunteers. Again, you will be approaching a targeted group of people who already show an interest in your congregation. Keep in mind that they don't want to be bombarded by requests to volunteer—just as they shouldn't be inundated with philanthropic requests via Facebook. But advertising opportunities from time to time can definitely help you as an additional marketing channel.

Don't be afraid to ask. In the same way you should never say no for a donor, never say no for a volunteer. You have no idea how much time a person does or does not have to volunteer for your congregation. Don't assume you do, even if she is your closest friend.

Understanding Different Types of Volunteers

Imagine for a minute that you could really figure out how to get each and every board member to participate in soliciting gifts for your annual fund. It is possible, if you consider what *participation* means and what you can expect from different types of volunteers.

There are a lot of different ways to categorize volunteers. The following list is not exhaustive; it is intended to help you consider where your volunteers' strengths and weaknesses lie. Each of us is a combination of these types, but who works well with whom and who complements whom among their fellow volunteers should be factors in developing various committees.

The "Organizer"

At some point each event needs someone who loves to organize, ideally paired with a Creative (see below). The Organizer makes sure the systems, checklists, spreadsheets, and job descriptions are all in place. He likes to be ahead of schedule but will take it a bit personally if there is lack of support or if others are unwilling to commit.

The "Creative"

Just as each event needs an Organizer at the top, each event also needs a Creative—but this person is best paired with someone who will keep the creativity focused and on schedule. Having too many Creatives working together can cause a lack of productivity or diversions in the schedule.

The "Busy, Busy, Busy"

Whether or not they are running the event, these volunteers have to be put in the busiest positions to remain interested. They are often committed to multiple nonprofits but manage to make a difference at everything they are involved in. It is worth getting them onboard before someone else signs them up.

The "Likes Name Recognition"

Similar to donors who need to see their names on buildings, rooms, benches, and the like, these volunteers want everyone to see that they are in charge, or at least helping out, in a visible manner. And just as you put the names of donors who like recognition in a prominent place, be sure to publicly recognize the contributions of these volunteers. It is an easy way to make a valuable volunteer more committed to your congregation.

The "Overcommitted" (aka the Person Who Thinks He Has More Time Than He Does)

This person understands the need for volunteers (oftentimes, he runs a few events himself) and always says yes to helping out. But because he spreads himself so thin, someone else has to pick up the slack when things don't go exactly as planned (and do they ever go exactly as planned?), he finds that another project (or work) is cutting into his volunteer hours, or he is facing a tight deadline he wasn't expecting. There are always times when volunteer commitments drop lower in priority than they should, but there are only so many apologies before the work needs to get done.

Knowing more about your volunteers—what type they are and who would work well with whom—will enable you to utilize them more effectively, both for their own good and for the benefit of your community.

It might be helpful to keep in mind that while personalities do not change overnight, there are times when each of us slips in and out of different "types." When our kids go off to school or college or our parents need more support, our ability to fulfill our commitments may ebb and flow. When it ebbs for your volunteers, be kind and remember that life happens for all of us. It may cause others on the development committee to have more work, but getting irritated and implying that someone is a bad volunteer will only leave a bad taste in everyone's mouth. Instead, ask for a realistic time frame for any tasks she has been assigned. If it is truly time-sensitive, ask if you can reassign some of her responsibilities in the short term. Make her feel appreciated and she will return to the fold. Leave her feeling ostracized and she will stop volunteering and stop donating—and that is true of even the most passionate volunteer.

Reading a Volunteer's Mind

It may come as a surprise to some of you that we encourage everyone to learn how to read a volunteer's mind as soon as he walks in the door and volunteers to help. Some of our clients are more successful at this than others. Below are some recommendations for the "others."

If you rely on volunteers to fulfill your mission, whether through committee work or day-to-day, mission-driven service, you should truly know each and every volunteer. That is, learn her reasons for volunteering and whether she has long-term goals within the organization, such as landing a job in the office or a seat on the board, or becoming a major donor.

Here is a guide to the four volunteer stages:

Stage 1: New Volunteer

When a volunteer first walks in the door or calls to see what opportunities are available, you are in the excitement period. Both parties are filled with the potential of the new relationship.

Best Way to Engage This Volunteer: Always ask each new volunteer to fill out a (relatively) simple form. Otherwise, you are missing a huge opportunity. Why? Because when he is interested enough to get involved, he will tell you something about himself before he sees whether or not he is well treated. (Not that you would intentionally mistreat anyone, but it happens.)

Important Questions to Ask: This is the time to find out the basic reasons that he came to offer his help. But that is only the start. You can find out his other interests, what aspects of volunteering appeals to him, whether he currently sits on any boards, whether he would ever consider sitting on your board, and anything else that can help you tailor his experience to your congregational needs.

Stage 2: The Semi-Experienced Volunteer

This is the volunteer who has been around for six to eighteen months on a regular basis. She understands the basics, has experience in a certain area, and now has a definite opinion of the congregation—whether positive or negative.

Best Way to Engage This Volunteer: Over a cup of coffee. This volunteer will give you more information in a casual conversation than she

WIN A $100 GIFT CERTIFICATE!

Fill in this card and mail it to us—
or fill it in **online** at

jewishlights.com/ feedback.html

—to be eligible for a $100 gift certificate for Jewish Lights books.

JEWISH LIGHTS PUBLISHING
SUNSET FARM OFFICES RTE 4
PO BOX 237
WOODSTOCK VT 05091-0237

Place
Stamp
Here

Fill in this card and return it to us to be eligible for our quarterly drawing for a $100 gift certificate for Jewish Lights books.

We hope that you will enjoy this book and find it useful in enriching your life.

Book title: _____

Your comments: _____

How you learned of this book: _____

If purchased: Bookseller _____ City _____ State _____

Please send me a free JEWISH LIGHTS Publishing catalog. I am interested in: (check all that apply)

1. ☐ Spirituality
2. ☐ Mysticism/Kabbalah
3. ☐ Philosophy/Theology
4. ☐ History/Politics

5. ☐ Women's Interest
6. ☐ Environmental Interest
7. ☐ Healing/Recovery
8. ☐ Children's Books

9. ☐ Caregiving/Grieving
10. ☐ Ideas for Book Groups
11. ☐ Religious Education Resources
12. ☐ Interfaith Resources

Name (PRINT) _____

Street _____

City _____ State _____ Zip _____

E-MAIL (FOR SPECIAL OFFERS ONLY) _____

Please send a JEWISH LIGHTS Publishing catalog to my friend:

Name (PRINT) _____

Street _____

City _____ State _____ Zip _____

JEWISH LIGHTS PUBLISHING

Tel: (802) 457-4000 • Fax: (802) 457-4004

Available at better booksellers. Visit us online at www.jewishlights.com

would ever write down now. Anecdotal information about her experiences can be invaluable.

Important Questions to Ask: What is the best part of your work with Congregation Emanuel? What is the part you like least? Are there other areas of the organization that interest you? Are there any ways you think that the volunteer experience could be improved?

Stage 3: The Experienced Volunteer

An experienced volunteer is someone who has been on a committee or volunteered within your congregation for more than eighteen months and understands its strengths and weaknesses.

Best Way to Engage This Volunteer: This person should be easy to approach. The more formal the interview process is at this point, the more information you will get. A casual meeting with this type of volunteer may often end up being a complaint session for a specific issue or drift into catching-up-with-a-friend mode. That is not to say that it shouldn't be friendly, but it should feel like a meeting with a stated, shared agenda.

Important Questions to Ask: Not to put too much pressure on you as a solicitor, but this meeting could make the difference between gaining a lifelong donor rather than just a long-term volunteer. Ask what he views as the strengths and weaknesses of the organization, if he is satisfied with his volunteering, whether or not he would ask friends to join him in volunteering, and even how he views the staff members. While this is far from a 360-degree review process, a volunteer is much more likely to list a staff member's best and worst qualities than a subordinate would.

Stage 4: Former Volunteer

If your organization utilizes volunteers, you have former volunteers. And those who left, on good or bad terms, hold valuable insights for your organization. Asking them to fill out a quick form will help you understand why you retain—or lose—volunteers each year. Then it is up to you to really listen to their responses and hear how to improve your retention rate.

Best Way to Engage This Volunteer: Online survey, email, or snail mail will all work, but keep the response mechanism easy, the entire form simple, and provide an option to offer opinions anonymously. A follow-up coffee or lunch may be a good way to steward these volunteers toward a major gift. You can explain that you do not know whether or not they filled out the form, but you would love anecdotal information to help the congregation improve.

Important Questions to Ask: In as few questions as possible, ask why she ended the relationship. Use this as an opportunity to get a good grasp of the situation and improve future experiences for other volunteers. Questions may include: Did you feel you were well employed as a volunteer? Was the work level what you expected? What are you most proud that you accomplished? What do you wish could have been accomplished? Would you recommend that a friend volunteer at the synagogue? Would you volunteer again for the synagogue? If so, would you like someone to contact you about other opportunities?

The Chairperson Dilemma

Choosing a development committee chairperson may be a controversial decision. Some will say, "Without question, one of the largest donors should be the chair." Others will say, "It has to be the person who is going to work the hardest to achieve our goals." Still others will say, "Let's get a few co-chairs. That will bring in the funding and make sure that at least one of them will work hard."

What's the right answer? Of course, there *is* no right answer. Fundraising is not a one-size-fits-all venture. If you are looking to dramatically improve your annual fund income (let's say, increase it by 50 percent), then you need to understand how your current and future infrastructure will determine whom you should choose for your chairperson.

Here's the chairperson's job description:

- He makes an exemplary leadership gift.
- He recruits members of the development committee and solicits gifts when and where appropriate.
- He sets the tone for committee work, ensures that members have the information they need to do their jobs, and oversees the logistics of the committee's operation. As the committee's link to the board, he frequently consults with and reports to the board chair.

- She reports to the full board on committee decisions, policy recommendations, and other committee business. She works closely with the rabbi and development staff person, if any, as well as other staff liaisons to the committee.
- She assigns work to committee members, sets meeting agendas and runs meetings, and ensures distribution of minutes and reports to members.
- She initiates and leads the committee's ongoing evaluation, a process in which committee members review their accomplishments in relation to the committee's work.

Once you have a few candidates to consider, work your way through the flowchart on the following pages.

Who Should Chair Your Development Committee?

If you have a staff member dedicated to fundraising ...

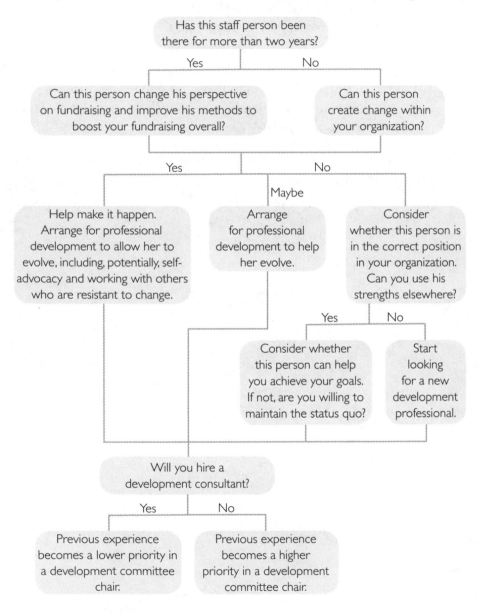

If you do not have a staff member dedicated to development …

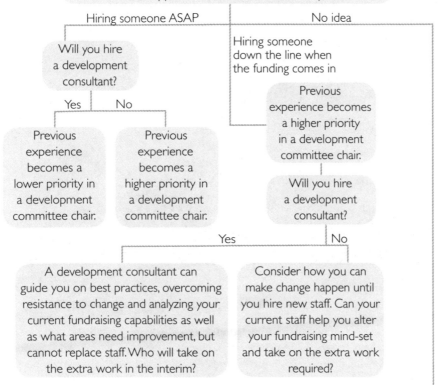

How do you plan to achieve additional impact when it comes to donor tracking, paperwork, follow-up, stewardship, and volunteer support without a dedicated staff person?

Hiring someone ASAP

No idea

Will you hire a development consultant?

Hiring someone down the line when the funding comes in

Yes | No

Previous experience becomes a higher priority in a development committee chair.

Previous experience becomes a lower priority in a development committee chair.

Previous experience becomes a higher priority in a development committee chair.

Will you hire a development consultant?

Yes | No

A development consultant can guide you on best practices, overcoming resistance to change and analyzing your current fundraising capabilities as well as what areas need improvement, but cannot replace staff. Who will take on the extra work in the interim?

Consider how you can make change happen until you hire new staff. Can your current staff help you alter your fundraising mind-set and take on the extra work required?

Determine whether you are ready for a new fundraising initiative. It may seem like a chicken-and-egg question, but if you gain new donors without additional support, you will end up angering donors and potentially decreasing your current funding levels.

Will you hire a development consultant?

Yes | No

A development consultant can guide you on best practices, overcoming resistance to change and analyzing your current fundraising capabilities as well as what areas need improvement, but cannot replace staff.

Consider how you can make change happen without changing your infrastructure or getting aid. Is your community ready for a change in your current fundraising model?

After working through the flowchart, list five possible candidates in order of how excited you would be to have them as the development committee chairperson:

1._____

2._____

3._____

4._____

5._____

For each one, consider:

Is this person a natural leader?

Is this person a major donor?

Is this person someone who does what he says he is going to do?

Is this person overcommitted? That is, will she make your synagogue a priority?

Is this person afraid or reluctant to ask someone for money?

Can you think of a natural partner for this person to balance both his skill sets and his temperament?

Does this person have a spouse who should co-chair? Would that be beneficial?

If you do not have a staff person specifically for development, you should also consider whether this volunteer is willing to do the work of a staff person, including donor tracking, paperwork, follow-up, stewardship, and volunteer support. If not, who will help this person achieve your new organizational goals?

Chapter 5

The Role of Clergy, Staff, and Volunteer Leadership in the Development Process

An essential aspect of any nonprofit enterprise that wants to survive, including the synagogue, is the development function.

A Board Member's Tasks and Responsibilities

Leadership, in this case volunteer leadership, trumps all. The board's support, follow-through, work ethic, determination, and understanding of their tasks and responsibilities will facilitate the success, or failure, of your undertaking in terms of reaching ambitious, new financial goals. The specific tasks and responsibilities of board members in the development and fundraising process are best remembered by the acronym GAINS.

The "G" in GAINS stands for "give." Each and every board member must make an exemplary gift over and above whatever dues and fees she may pay to be a member of the congregation. One hundred percent of the board should participate, because each of their gifts makes a difference. Additionally, their gifts empower them to serve as advocates and ambassadors to the other members of the congregation and to the community at large. And their gifts give them the credibility to fulfill their principal responsibility—to ask others to give.

The "A" in GAINS stands for "acknowledge." As we continually stress, stewardship is critical to the ongoing success of any development effort. The nonprofit community, in general, is facing a crisis when it comes to donor retention. And while the synagogue world may be different from other nonprofits, it is not exempt from this phenomenon.

In the past, it was possible to retain as many as 80 percent of donors who had made at least two contributions to an organization— particularly those who had contributed $250 or more. More recently, many nonprofits find that 80 percent number has been halved, and much of the reason for that is a failure to appreciate, acknowledge, and be accountable to donors who provide valuable philanthropic support.

Board members, especially, should be encouraged to acknowledge contributions in personally written letters and calls. As fiduciaries of the congregation, board members have the opportunity to tell donors how valuable their gift is and how it encourages them in their work as leaders and managers of the affairs of the synagogue. Board members should also seek out donors and greet them personally to express appreciation for the loyal support that each donor provides.

A simple program of asking board members to select three or four contributors from a list of donors who have given since the last time the board met will create an opportunity for feel-good calls that offer a thank-you and nothing more. If your congregation initiates such a program, you will distinguish yourselves from other nonprofits the donor supports. And you'll ensure the continued, faithful support of that donor.

The "I" in GAINS stands for "identify." The very beginning of the development cycle is the identification of prospective and existing donors. Every board member should participate in both group sessions and one-on-one meetings with development staff to identify and provide information about donors as well as prospects. We all wear many hats in our ever-increasingly complex lives. Board members know people who might be motivated and are definitely able to be philanthropically invested in the congregation, if they stop to consider it.

Whether it is through business or coaching a soccer team, through other nonprofit commitments or the sharing of sports or arts interests, we each know people—fellow or potential members of the congregation— who would support the programs and activities that enhance our Jewish lives and community. When you identify prospective donors you're not spending their money or giving it away for them; you are simply offering them the possibility of engagement and investment in a valuable organization.

The "N" in GAINS stands for "engage" or, if you prefer, "nurture." As a board member, you take on the responsibility of educating and encouraging prospects to financially support the congregation. There are a variety of ways to do this. Would you prefer to host a meeting for ten major gift prospects at your home or in the conference room in your office? Further along in this process of cultivation, you could offer one-on-one meetings to deepen the relationship with the prospects. Remember, fundraising and development are contact sports.

The "S" in GAINS stands for "solicit." This is the highest level of involvement that we can expect from a board member, and not every member will be willing to conduct personal, face-to-face solicitations. But those who do should be cherished.

Ultimately, people give to people, not to institutions. As such, you need people who are willing to engage in this type of conversation. You should only ask board members to approach people with whom they are comfortable. And when they do ask others to give, members fulfill their responsibility to provide financial resources and build a community of donors and funders.

The Role of Rabbinic Leadership

The rabbi of a congregation provides leadership in myriad ways—spiritually, intellectually, communally. In the area of financial resource development, the rabbi is a model for members of the board. As such, the same five roles that board members are asked and expected to undertake are also tasks fulfilled by the rabbi. In addition to being a Giver, an Acknowledger, an Identifier, an eNgager, and a Solicitor, the rabbi supports the volunteer leadership as well as staff colleagues in all they do to raise funds and to develop and manage relationships on behalf of the congregation. The rabbi is, optimally, the passionate articulator and embodiment of the congregational vision.

Sometimes the rabbi serves as a cheerleader to encourage those who directly lead and manage the development efforts. Other times, the rabbi may need to be a gentle "nudge" to help people do what they said they were going to do in the first place. And, of course, as in all matters, the rabbi is the educator and serves as the coach, not only to provide motivation but also to enhance skill development in the art and science of fundraising in the synagogue setting.

The rabbi can help celebrate with volunteer leaders and staff when victories large and small are achieved. Occasionally, the rabbi needs to commiserate when aspirations and expectations are unmet. Here it is crucial for the rabbi not to convey disappointment to the prospect or donor. As in all matters, the rabbi should engage with authenticity and integrity—key values for all to observe.

Staff with Development Responsibilities

Volunteers, while extremely valuable, can only achieve their goals with support from staff. Development requires consistency, organized documentation, and a central information clearinghouse to maintain the relationships required of a successful program.

Fundraising roles for staff include:

- Providing information about the congregation
- Developing proposals, letters, and other support materials
- Coordinating mailings of solicitation letters, sending emails, and maintaining a social media presence
- Following up on all solicitation calls
- Sending reminders and organizing report meetings
- Providing information about programs and tax advantages in a solicitation call
- Scheduling solicitation rehearsals

In the past decade or so, many congregations have hired staff to serve in development roles. If you have at least two hundred congregation members who have the financial capacity to make a gift of $5,000 or more, if properly motivated, then there is more than enough work for a full-time major gifts officer. If you have fewer than two hundred members who fall into that category, you still need development staff, but the person may be able to handle major gifts together with the annual fund. If you have a capital/endowment campaign on the horizon, you may require additional help. Before you say that you cannot afford dedicated staff, consider that the expense of a good development professional is an investment that can yield a return ten to fifteen times the cost on an annual basis by the third year of employment.

The Development Director

Here is a job description for a development director in the synagogue setting: The director of development will work as a member of the senior management team of the congregation. In consultation with the board, the director of development will design and implement a multi-year strategic plan to raise unrestricted annual funds, as well as programmatic endowment funds. In addition, the director will serve as the key staff person in the creation and implementation of a communications and media plan to increase the visibility of the congregation both internally and externally.

Among other specific responsibilities and duties, the director of development will do the following:

- Create and articulate the congregational case for giving (also known as a case statement or case for support; see chapter 9 for additional information).
- Develop a strategic fundraising plan that includes a time line, a gift table (indicating the number of gifts at various levels required in order to achieve the goal), and stewardship and communications programs.
- Prepare and monitor budgets for all development activities, subject to the approval of the board and the executive director.
- Coordinate and monitor all development activities of the congregation and regularly report results to the rabbi, the executive director, the development committee, and others, as required.
- Supervise the development of proposals for foundations and corporations.
- Design and implement a schedule for communicating with the various constituencies of the congregation.
- Motivate and lead board members to recognize and carry out their fundraising responsibilities.
- Identify and recruit additional members for the development committee and volunteer infrastructure for the congregation to expand the opportunities for major gift cultivation and solicitation.

- Train the board, development committee members, and volunteers to serve as solicitors and cultivators of other prospects.
- Create a system to support, track, and recognize volunteers.
- Supervise the research, cultivation, and development of appropriate solicitation strategies for identified and new major gift prospects.
- Engage in and direct personal solicitation of such prospects.
- Coordinate and conduct all communication with donors and prospective donors.
- Create a variety of appropriate gift vehicles to meet the needs of different donors.
- Administer stewardship activities by supervising the maintenance of the database of contributors and gifts; tracking current and potential donors; and acknowledging, recording, and reporting all gifts with appreciation to donors.
- Develop educational programs to support development efforts for major gifts, planned giving, and endowment funding on a local, regional, and national basis.
- Create a communication plan for donors and prospects, including reports from the director, brochures, and other communication tools that inform prospects and donors of special giving opportunities.

Finding the right person to fulfill the majority of these kinds of tasks is difficult. Experienced development professionals with a passion for the synagogue and the future of Jewish life are rare and, when discovered, are highly prized. A successful candidate for such a position is usually:

- An experienced professional with a proven track record in major gift solicitation and experience working with high-level volunteers and philanthropists.
- A strong leader and manager who is a self-starter and who listens and is able to build a motivated team of volunteers and staff.
- A hands-on director with superior verbal and written communication skills.
- A creative, energetic, bold, innovative, and dynamic individual, committed to realizing the potential of the congregation to enhance the Jewish community.

While the director of development provides management of the process, in a synagogue setting the rabbi is responsible for leadership. Consider the differences between leadership and management.

- Managers take care of the congregation's resources (financial, human, physical, and the like). Leaders ensure that the resources are being deployed in the best way.
- Managers are in charge of other people doing their jobs. Leaders provide guidance and assistance.
- Managers deal with situations as they occur. Leaders examine the situation to see if it is part of a pattern that can be addressed and how the situation affects others in the organization.
- Managers tell others what to do. Leaders use communication to encourage others to achieve the organization's goals.
- Managers do what they are supposed to do. Leaders do what should be done.
- Managers ensure that deadlines are met and work gets done. Leaders consider what will motivate the staff or volunteers to help meet the deadline and what might stand in the way.
- Managers know the correct way to get a job done. Leaders recognize that other people sometimes have good ideas and listen to the possibilities.
- Leaders are the innovators, the motivators, the people we all want to work for and with.

Chapter 6

What All Fundraisers Need to Know

Habits of a Successful Fundraiser

What makes a successful fundraiser? This is a difficult question to answer because each congregation is different and each prospective donor will react differently to a solicitor. There are, however, certain general habits of highly successful synagogue fundraisers that you can incorporate into your routine. In fact, we will go so far as to say that integrating these behaviors into your personal toolkit will have remarkable results in your fundraising and your life.

For instance, your next encounter with a major gift prospect will have the greatest chance at success if you are well prepared, so you can guide the conversation to the best possible conclusion. The conclusion may be a major gift or it may be setting up the next appointment. Either way, know what your ideal goal is, what other outcomes would make you feel successful, and what you can do to ensure optimal results. Here are some habits to cultivate to make yourself a successful fundraiser:

Habit #1: Ask the right questions. Ease in with simple questions that get the prospect talking about himself, and then move on. It is your responsibility to keep the conversation moving forward.

Habit #2: Be engaging. Plan topics to potentially touch on, but work from the unique set of verbal and nonverbal cues your prospect gives you. Discuss the surroundings. Talk about the people you both know. Encourage a comfortable conversation that feels natural. Urge the prospect to begin to talk about herself. Show you care by really caring.

Habit #3: Take the lead. Tell the prospect where you are in the campaign. Don't be afraid to steer the conversation toward the reason you are there. You both know why you are sitting together. Invite questions or concerns along the way; that gives you an opportunity to have the kind of honest conversation that can lead to a gift. Of course, a calm, professional manner is essential—no matter how the prospect reacts.

Habit #4: Communicate credibility. Don't cut corners at the expense of your own credibility—it's one of the most powerful weapons you have. You're not in the business of attracting suckers or conveying false impressions to get the gift; you are in the business of building a mutually beneficial, long-term partnership.

Habit #5: Tell the truth (it's easier to remember). As a follow-up to communicating credibility, be honest. According to "Looking Good and Lying to Do It" by Brent Weiss and Robert S. Feldman, the most commonly referenced study on honesty in the past ten years, the average person will lie two to three times in a ten-minute conversation. (Incidentally, women tend to lie to make the other person feel better, while men tend to lie to make themselves look better.) Is it wrong to tell someone you love her home when you really think the décor is totally tasteless? Probably not, but do not mislead the prospect about your ability to meet a deadline or where you are in the campaign. Remember, the truth always comes out.

Habit #6: Don't pretend you know it all. When you hit a bump in the conversation—a question you can't answer or a concern that you don't know how to respond to, don't improvise and make something up. Tell the prospect that you will look into it and want to come back with a response. Solving problems and overcoming hurdles are par for the course and you have to listen, consider, and often confer with others before you can come up with a solution.

Habit #7: Take notes. Taking notes during your meeting with a prospect helps you listen, puts you in a position of authority, encourages your prospect to open up, and sends positive signals that you are really interested in what she is saying.

Habit #8: Create a plan specific to each new prospect. Ideally, this will become routine for you. It will help frame the conversation, what is unique about this situation, and define your goal for each meeting. Seasoned donors will know what to expect from you. They will expect that you are organized and have a plan. Also, it will enable you to produce a customized, written plan, based on your notes from earlier meetings, to share with the committee and put in the prospect's file.

Habit #9: Show enthusiasm and optimism. Talk up your organization. But keep in mind that there is a difference between enthusiasm and poorly disguised panic. Enthusiasm builds bridges; panic and fear of failure tear them down.

Habit #10: Ask for referrals. Don't be shy—you can't afford it. Referrals are the lifeblood of a successful fundraising program. Be direct and say, "I'm willing to bet there are people you know who might also want to support the synagogue. Do you know five people I could talk to?"

Habit #11: Ask for the next appointment on the first visit. This is perhaps the simplest, easiest-to-follow piece of advice. Don't make excuses—make appointments. If you leave without setting up a definite follow-up meeting, you will have to go back and forth to reschedule, wasting time for both of you. You can always blame the committee: "They expect me to come back with an appointment, so would you mind helping me stay in their good graces?"

Habit #12: Give yourself appropriate credit. Talk about yourself, but be humble. (The two are not mutually exclusive.) Convey success, confidence, and flexibility. Highlight your past successes, but don't try to one-up the prospect. Try to exhibit the characteristics of a person who makes things happen.

Habit #13: Sell yourself on yourself. Motivate yourself! Have you ever considered listening to motivational podcasts? Or follow Eric Thomas or Tony Robbins on social media to get inspired on a regular basis. Do whatever you need to in order to remember that one of the keys to success is to specify your goals—and your rewards (ideally, writing them down). Get positive reinforcement. Leave yourself notes and always, always keep things in perspective.

Habit #14: Start early. There is a world before 9:00 a.m.! You can ease your commute, reduce your aggravation, and improve your attitude by getting to work an hour or so before everyone else does. That extra hour can be used to write handwritten thank-you notes to donors, prepare materials for solicitors, and update fundraising progress reports. It may sound tough, but try it anyway. You'll be a convert before you know it.

Do You Want to Change the Way You Fundraise?

The person who goes farthest is generally the one who is willing to do and dare. The sure-thing boat never gets far from shore.

—Dale Carnegie

If you're not asking them for money, someone else is.

—Abigail Harmon

Recently, a few friends have expressed frustration when their congregation told them not to ask certain donors for money. The excuses vary, but included:

- "The board has decided that this is not the kind of synagogue that asks people for specific amounts." This is usually followed by "This has always worked for us in the past."
- "The Cohens are potential donors but the development team feels that they have not been members long enough to ask them for anything substantial."
- "We're not sure the Bernsteins are involved enough yet to ask for the kind of money they have the potential to donate."
- "We want to ask Joe Baer for a major gift next year so we don't want to ask him for a small gift this year."
- _____[Fill this in with a reason you just heard to *not* ask for a gift.]

Then there are the stall tactics:

- "I'm not sure we have a strong enough case."
- "We need to create a plan for this type of donor. As soon as we get through ____ [fill in the blank with the next holiday, event, vacation], we will make it one of our priorities."
- "Let's look at all the prospective donors and what we should do about them at the next meeting."

Reversing the Trend

If you have a new prospect who joined the congregation within the past year and you are developing a plan of action, determining how to get that prospective donor more involved, and deepening your personal relationship with her, don't listen to what follows. You are on the right track.

For everyone else reading this, it's time to change the way you fundraise.

The often quoted definition of insanity is "doing the same thing over and over again and expecting different results." It is time to stop the insanity when you consider your fundraising efforts. What would change the results this year—why would this year be different from all other years? Do you think this year will be the year that you uncover new prospect information? That your leadership will be ready to approach donors in a new and different way? Will something change in the way a particular member is engaged? Will something change in the way the development team works or the fundraising committee functions?

Stopping the cycle of insanity means that shifts—sometimes cataclysmic in size and impact—need to be made if you expect to dramatically improve your fundraising results.

An Honest Look

It is time to determine where you are going to find the time, resources, and leadership to change your current structure. Who will take responsibility for initiating the change? How will you pay for the necessary prospect research or fundraising software? Who will oversee the stewardship and cultivation of prospects? And what else needs to change for you to achieve your goals?

We consultants are often called in to ask the questions that you have been—and should no longer be—avoiding. And now is the time for you to ask yourself these questions. If you are on the fence about whether or not you need to do something drastic, consider these questions:

- How long will it be until you run through your endowment?
- How long have you been running a deficit?
- How do you currently handle the deficit?

- Which is more important to your congregation—keeping a low-key culture where money is not discussed or ensuring the achievement of the mission and the fulfillment of the vision?
- Are you truly looking for a solution or are you merely hoping that someone will ride in to save the day with a quick fix?

Take an honest look at your congregation. Are you ready to learn how to improve your synagogue culture, make development the cornerstone of everything you do, and ensure that your synagogue will be on stable ground for years to come? Are you ready to change the way you fundraise?

Personal and Professional Development

Training is not a sign of weakness, but rather a sign that you know your strengths lie elsewhere. When you are considering pursuing fundraising and development training for personal or professional reasons, you are taking the first step toward improving yourself and your congregation.

For Staff

The skills necessary for a development professional—or someone who is charged with development responsibilities, even if he also holds another position—are vast. Looking at the list that follows, are there areas that you know need improvement? Do you have in-depth knowledge of the following?

- The fundraising campaign strategy?
- How to establish, monitor, and evaluate goals, benchmarks, and performance?
- How to engage in and direct personal solicitation of prospects for major and planned gifts?
- How to motivate and lead board members in development activities?
- Donor communications?
- Stewardship activities and tracking, including the maintenance of the database of contributors and gifts, tracking current and potential donors, acknowledgment and recognition vehicles, and recording and reporting of all gifts?
- The fundraising events that are currently being run?

Can you do the following?

- Develop a strategic fundraising plan that identifies opportunities for fundraising and stewardship of major gifts prospects?
- Conduct donor research and help identify, cultivate, and steward potential new major and planned gift donors, as well as establish donor cultivation and donor stewardship recognition strategies?
- Create a compelling case for support of the synagogue?
- Work with a development committee?
- Supervise the research, cultivation, and development of appropriate solicitation strategies for identified and new major gift prospects?
- Engage in and direct personal solicitation of such prospects?
- Provide or arrange for training for staff, board members, and volunteer leadership to serve as solicitors and cultivators of other prospects?
- Supervise the writing of and/or write proposals for individuals, foundations, and corporations?
- Prepare and monitor budgets for all development activities?
- Develop educational programs to support efforts for major gifts, planned giving, and endowment funding on a local, regional, and national basis?

For Volunteers

A volunteer is not the same as a staff person and should not be used as such, but we all know that volunteers are often asked to pick up the slack where appropriate staff resources are lacking. A strong development committee member will have a deep knowledge of the following:

- The synagogue's mission, vision, and goals
- The development committee and volunteer infrastructure, including the current methods of identifying and recruiting additional members
- The annual campaign, including direct mail, emails, personal solicitations, and fundraising events
- The fundraising target and the fundraising plan to achieve those goals
- How to partner with the development staff to support their congregational priorities

- The balance between fundraising sources—not relying too heavily on any one person, foundation, or event
- How to create and carry out stewardship and solicitation plans for all major donors
- The board's fiscal and fiduciary responsibility

Volunteer and staff roles are not the same. While both require support and some of the skill sets overlap, if you need training, consider the specific type of education that will help your congregation achieve fiscal sustainability and/or your new fundraising goals. And then consider having the staff and volunteers learn side by side.

Fundraising Is a Marathon, Not a Sprint

Fundraising is a long race. Ideally, it's even longer than a marathon—it is a lifetime relationship that goes beyond the donor's need for the services that a synagogue can offer in any given year. The affiliation is not a placeholder until donors need pastoral care, have children in need of religious school, or are searching for someone to officiate at the wedding of a child. The marathon metaphor also works because you associate those 26.2 miles with hard work and time invested that offer amazing feelings and a realization that you accomplished something substantial. Now, multiply those feelings by the number of member families. Ready to get your sneakers on?

It's Harder to Get the Appointment Than to Get the Gift

The reason fundraising professionals are often called development professionals is not because the organization is trying to trick people with a less scary name for the function. Fundraising is about developing relationships with individuals, foundations, corporations, and the general public. In a synagogue, a long-term relationship must go beyond one rabbi, High Holiday seats, or the b'nai mitzvah education.

The goal is to encourage each family unit to be connected to the community for all stages of their life, their children's lives, and potentially their grandchildren's lives. The long-term commitment is akin to a marriage, a place to go to in times of joy and sadness, providing a lifetime support system, and giving you a sense of security while allowing for personal growth.

Then giving to the synagogue is an organic way to preserve their current experience and ensure that future generations will be able to worship, learn, and experience community within the same walls (or new and improved walls after a capital campaign—after all, this is a fundraising book).

A successful campaign—whether annual, capital, or endowment—requires your solicitors to understand the nuances of stewardship (see chapter 15).

Among other things, a successful solicitor will:

- Look to develop a long-term relationship with the donor(s)
- Offer a strong case for giving
- Practice what she is going to say and how she is going to say it
- Understand how to overcome objections
- Establish follow-through mechanisms
- Believe that he will be successful

We have taught many, many people how to achieve their financial goals. But we are always happily surprised when someone asks the seemingly simple yet ultimately essential follow-up question. It can come in many forms, but a classic version is this: "So do I just pick up the phone and start calling these people?"

As long as you have a plan. Successful solicitation is, in large part, a matter of preparation, including how a solicitor can get the face-to-face meeting with the donor in the first place. Some long-term donors make it very easy for you and respond to your first call with potential meeting times. But others give you such a hard time that you'll start to wonder if this donor is worth the effort.

A prospective donor's resistance to arranging for a meeting in no way correlates to his ability or willingness to become a major donor.

The following are some tips that will help you get the meeting:

- Prepare a script and practice, practice, practice.
- State upfront that you would be happy to come to her home whenever it would be convenient for her (an office is a second but less ideal option).
- Ask whether his spouse would be present.

- Offer two specific times on two different days of the week, as in "Would you like to meet on Tuesday at 3:00 or would Thursday at 10:00 be better for you?"
- If neither of those days works, offer another pair. And if that does not work, ask whether a morning, afternoon, or evening would be best.
- Ask whether a workday or weekend would be preferable and then offer additional options.
- If a spouse will be present, ask when you should call back to check if the suggested times work (give options).

In general, be prepared to ask questions in which you offer a choice of answers, not just a yes or no. Try not to accept, "Can I think about it and get back to you?" You know how busy this person is and how hard it is to get back to someone—especially someone who is going to ask for money at some point. Make it as easy as possible to finalize a meeting time by asking when you can get back to her. If the person asks if this about giving money, always be honest. But remember that a good solicitor is not only going to ask about a donation. "Sure, I would like to speak with you about your contribution to Congregation Emanuel, but not only your monetary contribution. We want to talk to you about how you feel about the congregation and what aspects of it interest you. We want to hear your opinions about how we are doing and where we should be heading."

It may not be a conscious thought, but few people want to give substantially to any organization without having their voice heard. Letting a prospective donor know that you want to hear his thoughts will make him more receptive to the conversation.

Remember that you are representing your congregation—a place you value. Determine how you would like to be treated and keep that in mind at all times. And don't forget patience. It is one of the successful solicitor's strongest tools.

Chapter 7

When to Call in the Consultants

Does Your Annual Fund Need Professional Help?

Do you *need* to hire a consultant? Do you *want* to hire a consultant? Has a board member *required* you to hire a consultant?

Consultants cost money. Let's get that out of the way right off the bat. But how do you know if you need to hire someone to help your fundraising process? Here are some of the questions you might consider when determining whether or not to hire a consultant.

- Do you need dramatically different results from your fundraising?
- Are you ready for a cultural shift in the way you look at fundraising? Do you need someone to highlight how you can alter the way you fundraise in order to achieve remarkably different results?
- Will the board be open to doing things differently?
- Will there be resistance to asking all board members for financial support?
- Is the person who would lead this change able to influence the board?
- Does the person in charge understand development and fundraising techniques for a synagogue annual fund?
- Does this person have the right temperament to lead your board through the changes?
- Is this person able to articulate a plan and time line for the process?

P.S. This list can also be used when you are interviewing consultants to know if you are talking to the right one for your congregation.

Additional Considerations

Still unsure if you should hire a consultant or an additional dedicated fundraising staff member? Envision this: You have decided to grow a few vegetables in your backyard. You get so excited when you realize you have ten-plus flowers that promise cucumbers on your plant. You can farm! Congratulations!

So, are you ready to grow one hundred plants or one thousand?

It turns out that farming is like fundraising. And not just in a "tend it and it will grow" kind of way, although that is true.

Instead, think about how you got this far with your one plant. You can cobble together advice from a garden store and various websites. You can get the right soil for the containers, the right organic fertilizer for vegetables, and remember to water them most days. And that's awesome on a small scale. But if you want anything substantial, anything that would feed a family or sustain a nonprofit, you need an expert.

You can hire one, consult with one, or go to school to become one, but you need an expert to thrive on a larger scale.

Continuing this metaphor, we could go as far as to say that if you are raising most of your money from a few time-consuming events and a Yom Kippur appeal, you are a home gardener. If you are getting all that you need, then you are doing what works for your congregation. But, if your synagogue is barely breaking even or tapping into the principal of your reserves, it is time to expand by gaining a greater understanding of how development works.

It is easy to say that there is no money for a consultant or new staff. But there is no money because you are only doing the basics. Break the cycle and transform your results.

How can you pay for a consultant or specialist who can help you make substantial improvements to your annual fund? Consider these moves as potential next steps:

- Solicit a single funder or several donors to help you pay for two years of a part-time development professional.
- Find a funder to help you hire a consultant for six months to help you chart the right path for your organization.
- Take classes at a local university to sharpen your development and management skills.

- Engage a skilled development professional who will volunteer to train you and your staff once a month—with homework in between. (This may be ideal but is extremely hard to find.)
- Bring on board a skilled development professional from the congregation who will have the time to train your staff and his fellow volunteers. (Remember that skilled professionals who volunteer for your congregation still have a job to do to pay the bills.)
- _____

[Fill in your idea here]

There are many ways to find the funding to engage help, but take the time now to determine where you want to head. Indecision is a decision, but rarely to the benefit of any organization, especially a congregation.

That container garden seems easier and easier, doesn't it?

Justifying Your Costs to the Board

Do you know the old saying, it takes money to make money? Do you know why it's a famous saying? Because investing in your company, nonprofit, or, more specifically, your religious institution is required to make more money. The consulting costs are one aspect, but there is also the cost of the fundraising software, the staff person's time (as well as other allocated costs), and/or marketing materials.

Many synagogues have been bootstrapping to get things accomplished for as long as anyone can remember. Need a mailer sent out? Call in the volunteers. Someone's on vacation or on medical leave at a critical time? Let's call the former board president to help cover some of the work (after all, she knows how the whole place works). Need to raise more money? The current board president and fundraising committee chair can do it. (The fact that they work as a doctor and an insurance company executive, respectively, is irrelevant; they should be able to do it because they are the board president and the fundraising committee chair.)

Can the board president and the fundraising committee chair determine whether the congregation needs an organizational assessment, development audits, or a staff assessment? Will they be able to craft a new development plan, prospect research, solicitor training, strategic planning, and an annual fund enhancement strategy? If not, you may want to bring in a consultant or hire a full-time development profes-sional who is capable of doing these tasks. Most importantly, will the rest of your board allow an "insider" to share his expertise in a way that will impact your congregation?

All the recommendations in the world are irrelevant if your board and volunteer leadership are unwilling to provide the time and energy necessary to make the changes required for success, including hiring new development staff or retaining a consultant. Can the board presi-dent and/or the fundraising committee chair move the board out of complacency? This is the time to be honest with yourself. Failed cam-paigns erode morale well beyond the fundraising committee.

PART III

Tools for Donor Engagement

Chapter 8

Where Will You Find Your Donors?

Prospect Research

Prospect research largely comes from two sources. The first is external research or data that you can purchase from companies that specialize in collecting public records. The second is internal research that your development committee knows about their friends, family, and colleagues. Both are invaluable to the success of your fundraising campaign. Let's look at what each resource can offer you.

External Prospect Research

With more information publicly available than ever before, understanding prospect research has become a highly sophisticated and increasingly significant tool for nonprofit organizations. This is true whether you are looking to retain donors or to broaden the reach of your fundraising.

The complex analysis offered by a prospect research company can help you identify who has the capacity, as well as the inclination, to give to your congregation. This kind of research enables you to identify a congregation's best prospective new donors, as well as better understand how to approach each one of your existing donors to request an increased donation.

Some congregational leaders shy away from prospect research because they believe that it is too intrusive. However, professional prospect researchers—those who abide by the code of ethics of the Association for Prospect Researchers for Advancement (APRA), for example—use only publicly available information accessible to anyone. Prospect researchers must balance an individual's right to privacy with the needs of their client institutions to collect, analyze, record, maintain, use, and disseminate information. The key difference is that professionals do it efficiently and economically.

Additionally, prospect research helps:

- Start and develop relationships
- Identify prospective donors who share your congregation's values
- Uncover "hidden" donors
- Increase gifts from existing donors
- Plan approach and engagement strategies
- Determine each donor's capacity to give as well as a potential gift amount
- Determine the ask amount
- Formulate ask strategies
- Categorize donors by likelihood of giving, capacity to give, and type of gift (annual, major, planned)
- Identify potential board members and congregation champions
- Build guest lists for events
- Efficiently use fundraising/development resources
- Reduce fundraising costs

The most important predictor of a donor's likelihood to give is past philanthropy. Statistically, it is the best predictor of future behavior. In addition, there is a strong correlation between political giving, as reported by the Federal Elections Commission (FEC), and charitable giving: a donor who has made multiple political gifts totaling $15,000 or more has almost certainly made at least a five-figure gift to a nonprofit.

Additionally, understanding professionally provided prospect research can uncover shared interests and engagement strategies, and help you find hidden connections between your donors and your congregation's leaders. This can benefit the annual fund, but it can also deepen the relationship of a member with the congregation.

This new knowledge will help formulate an ask strategy. For example, a prospect may have a relatively low income but large amounts of real estate. By discreetly introducing real estate into the conversation and providing examples of real estate gifts, that donor can be persuaded to make a larger gift than one based on income alone. Enabling the donor to give a meaningful gift to the congregation—without laying out cash, which would be a hardship for him—will feel amazing. No one will give you more than he is willing to give, no matter what your relationship or what knowledge you possess. You, as a solicitor, are using prospect research to guide your synagogue and the donor to the best possible outcome.

The other aspect of prospect research to consider is the old 80/20 rule: 80 percent of your gifts will come from 20 percent of your prospects. (Now, as we mentioned earlier, the ratio is often closer to 90/10.) By identifying the 20 percent of your prospects who are most likely to make significant gifts to your congregation, you can focus your efforts and maximize your development efficiency.

How does it work? First, you provide a prospect research firm with the database of your members with their giving history to the congregation, the date and amount of their first, latest, and largest gifts, as well as the total number and aggregate amount of their gifts. The firm scans giving records and histories from every possible source and then compares your congregation's members or prospects to the databases of data they have assembled. As a result, the firm provides detailed snapshots for everyone listed in these records.

Each of your donors will have his or her own record, which you can sort based on any number of criteria, but most often congregations go straight to who, on their prospect list, has the largest capacity to give. Again, keep in mind that the amount of information may feel a bit intrusive at first glance, and absolutely overwhelming in the aggregate. But it is public information when someone buys or sells a house or gives to a candidate for public office, so what you see is a relatively clinical report.

In order to get an accurate picture of a prospect, you have to look at each category through a critical lens.

- Real estate holdings. Is her wealth based largely on real estate? Look more closely. Is it based on one property or more? Are there two vacation homes or is one a rental property? And how does each help you assess her capacity to give to your campaign?
- Does he tend to give $10,000 to multiple organizations or $50,000 to one specific organization each year?

- What is the largest gift she has given?
- Is there a certain type of organization that he has supported in the past? What do you know about these organizations?
- Have there been SEC-reported holdings uncovered of large amounts of publicly traded securities?
- What is her capacity range, based on her past philanthropy and her wealth?

Internal Prospect Research

Once you have the giving history and the prospect research record in hand, it is time to consider what the development committee knows about each prospect. Sorting your findings to focus on the aforementioned 80/20 rule will help you get a short list of first-tier prospects. Those close to the prospects will be able to look through the list and know whether a particular assessment is accurate or whether they are missing critical facts that could never be found in public records.

Only someone close to them would know that:

- The Goldsteins have two homes in Florida on their profile because they have been unable to sell their first house when they purchased their second.
- The Jacobs had a recent death in the family that could mean a substantial inheritance.
- Jonah Karmizan is taking on the financial support of an elderly parent.
- And, perhaps most importantly, do these first-tier prospects feel close to the synagogue and are they ready to make a gift or do they need more cultivation to feel valued?

This is not looking for gossip. This is guiding you toward a clear understanding of a prospect to know where he fits into the overall fundraising strategy. And while it may feel strange engaging in this kind of conversation about your friends, this information should only be used in a confidential manner and not be considered public knowledge by anyone.

Remember, to achieve the most from your fundraising campaign, you have to be armed with the best possible information from every resource you can access.

Confidentiality Issues

In the last chapter, when considering prospective volunteers, we briefly discussed confidentiality concerns. Knowing who should and will see data about the members of the congregation is an extremely important decision and one that should not be made lightly. Even a seemingly minor breach of confidentiality can have a ripple effect throughout your fundraising efforts. It is always better to be safe than sorry.

So who should be allowed access to information about donors? (You know the players involved, so remember that these are guidelines and not hard-and-fast rules.)

Campaign chairs are on the top of the list. They are charged with orchestrating a (potentially complicated) set of individual fundraising plans, solicitation strategies, and stewardship moves. This cannot be done without the full knowledge of each person being discussed. It also aids the chair in making solicitor assignments. At first the assignments may be purely based on the relationships of the solicitor and the prospect, but over time there will be people who shine at encouraging "stretch gifts" or overcoming the anxieties of longtime members. This can then be taken into account.

Committee members should see the entire list of prospect names in order to highlight those each one knows personally, but not necessarily the list with prospect research data included. Having more than one version of the list will make it easier to share appropriately.

The committee can offer personal knowledge, including major life cycle events in the recent past or near future, familial changes, current financial status (as well as whether or not it has recently changed or will soon change), who is most likely to make the financial decision about the gift to the synagogue, and whether a person feels good about his relationship with the congregation.

It may seem overwhelming, but you will only understand the true capacity of the list when you find out this information for each and every family unit, even if you have eight hundred members.

The development committee chair or the development staff will collect the information and create a more accurate picture of the prospects. Then it is time to bring a small, confidential group together to "rate" the list of prospects. This rating will determine who should be on each tier of members to be solicited. A list of people on these tiers—A, B, C, and D, without the financial information—can be returned to the committee-at-large to assign the best person to be the primary solicitor. Then the information on that individual or family will be provided to the solicitor—no one else on the committee.

While the committee may never see the full results, you will need to ask the entire development committee to provide this prospect information. Even those intimately involved in the synagogue will only know a small portion of people and a smaller portion of the information that can help form ratings.

Clergy

The rabbi(s) and cantor should be involved in this process. They can be very helpful in solicitations, but never ask your clergy to breach the confidentiality of a congregant. Instead, the clergy should be encouraged to use language that will enable them to feel good about providing information that will help you achieve the fundraising goals. You might consider:

- "That gift will not be possible this year. I'd rather not say why." No explanation given or necessary.
- "This is not the time to ask them." Respect the suggestion and put the prospect on the list to be discussed again in six months or a year.
- "They are in a good place right now and you should initiate the conversation soon." You may not know what has changed financially, but it will give you greater confidence in moving forward with an increased gift ask.

One caveat: At times, clergy may be conservative in whom to ask or not ask. Unlike that of an executive director, a clergyperson's original job description does not call for being a strong fundraiser. When asking the rabbi or cantor to participate, you should explain that you are not encouraging clergy to say no for donors, simply to provide information that will help you avoid embarrassing a donor or making anyone feel uncomfortable. Giving should feel good!

Staff

Staff are essential in every step of your new fundraising campaign. You will need people to help document, organize, update, and supply prospect research. They will also be able to make suggestions while keeping confidential issues private. If you do not think the staff can walk the line of giving information and understanding confidentiality issues, they may not be in the right job.

Improving Your Odds

Prospect research improves your odds by giving you the most information you can gather before you even begin to think about scheduling a meeting. The following list will help you know if you have the information you need to move forward.

Past Giving History

Do you know:

- To what nonprofits this prospect has given?
- How much she has given each year to each organization?
- How many years she has given to each nonprofit?
- Why she gives to each nonprofit? (For instance, is her best friend the executive director? Did her father have Alzheimer's disease? Is she passionate about food insecurity and a volunteer with that organization?)

Current Financial Situation

Consider these points:

- Has his financial capacity changed recently or will it change in the foreseeable future?
  - Is he buying or selling a house?
  - Is he contemplating new or different employment?
  - Is a child starting college?
  - Is a parent ill?
- Does the prospect see himself as financially secure and able to make a gift?
- Is he philanthropic by nature?

Relationship with the Congregation

- How does she feel about the synagogue? Is it a place to be used solely for life cycle events or does she feel a part of the community?
- Does she currently give to the annual campaign? And does she give the minimum or does she understand the financial commitment necessary to support the institution?
- Is there only one point of connection (a rabbi or the preschool) or is she involved in many ways?
- Are her friends involved as well?
- How often does she come into the building for services, classes, or special events?
- Are there ways in which you could see her getting more involved?

It is no coincidence that the list describing a prospect's relationship to the synagogue is the longest. Just because someone has the capacity to give does not mean he has the inclination to give *to you*. His relationship with the synagogue—whether that is through the clergy, services, lifelong learning, or his friendships—will be the best indicator as to the level of gift he is willing to give when compared to his capacity.

Analyzing the Data

Once you have created a profile of each of your prospects, it is sometimes a bit stunning to find out a member's capacity. While respecting their confidentiality, what do you do with all this data? You analyze it to determine the appropriate ask amount.

There is no exact formula to define the right amount to ask for in a face-to-face solicitation. A lot of what we consider is how donors like this have performed in the past. If you do not have this kind of information, remember a few rules:

- If you ask for too much, they may laugh, they may be flattered, or they may be shocked, but they will keep that amount in their minds as a starting point.
- If you ask for too much by an amount that they feel is so far beyond their willingness or capacity to give, they will give you the amount that they already had in mind when you walked in the door.

- If they offer you an amount that is much smaller than you had hoped, you do not have to immediately say thank you and move on to other topics of conversation. You can say something like this: "We appreciate that but, as you know, we were hoping for a bit more. Would you consider giving $X,XXX [an amount equal to 150 percent of the amount they offered]? We are really looking for each member to give a little extra this year to help establish new programs or fulfill a matching gift [have something specific in mind for this prospect]." Or ask, outright, if there is any way they could see themselves increasing this gift. Then thank them for their generosity. You always want people to feel good about their gift and how it will help the congregation.

- Remember that whether or not they give, or give as much as you ask them to, has little to do with you. Do not take it personally (see page 37).

- If they immediately say okay, the number in their head was probably larger than what you asked for. Try making a joke about it and see if you can increase the gift. Whether they increase it or not, be respectful and filled with gratitude for their participation in the campaign.

- Be gracious, no matter the results. You are representing yourself and the synagogue. Giving should help members feel closer to the synagogue and that they are helping the community. They should never leave a meeting feeling bad for not donating or giving less than you had hoped.

- The amount for which you are asking is an educated guess. Do not be hard on yourself for being hopeful and coming in under your ask. Optimism will help throughout the process, including when you're making the next call.

Chapter 9

The Case for Giving

The case for giving is a document that clearly explains and inspires a prospect to donate to your congregation for this campaign. A synagogue's need is not a compelling reason in and of itself. If you disagree, take out a piece of paper and consider every nonprofit that is in need, from international NGOs to local family service agencies. The list could probably fill pages. Anyone can make a case for need. Instead, explain why giving to *your* synagogue during this campaign will enable the donor to make a difference and change lives through her support, because the congregation enables the community to accomplish X, Y, and Z.

The Essential Elements

To make a successful ask, whether you are talking to an individual, a corporate giving officer, or a foundation program person, you need to have a good story that humanizes the congregation, its specialness, and why it is a great investment.

The Setup: Know the Background to Move Forward

Every person who is going to tell the story should know when the congregation was founded, what makes it special, and how it has evolved since its inception. While you should always have written materials to support your endeavor and to leave behind for the donor to consider, the solicitor is the one who makes the case first. The essence of a good story can and should be used by executive directors, board members, and grant writers alike.

Talking Through the Case for Giving

What do you need to prepare to talk about?

Your mission. The storyteller should be able to articulate the mission and vision as well as the purpose of this synagogue in this community.

Current programs. It is important to know and be able to respond to questions about the programs and services that the congregation offers, why they are special, and how they help fulfill the community's needs.

Current status of the budget. If you are continually on, over, or under budget, people want to know. If you cannot answer the basic finance questions, you can't ask people to increase their gift or support the congregation with a first-time gift.

The anecdote. What anecdotes can you tell that will spur conversation, interest, and donations? Was there something specific that brought you to the congregation? Is there a tale you could tell about something that recently happened while you were at the temple? (This also shows that you are personally involved and invested in the outcome of the fundraising campaign.) Did you recently discover some new aspect of the program that affected you on a personal level (maybe even encouraged you to take on this leadership role)?

You don't want this to sound canned, but planning is essential to successful development and a story is no different. Think of the general concepts ahead of time, but choose the specific details based on what you hear from the prospective donor so that he knows you are listening to him. Moreover, it will contribute to an impromptu, more natural exchange. Caution: If the tale feels old to you, it will feel old to the prospect. So, unlike a mission or vision, stories need to change on a regular basis.

The future. Be able to articulate your vision for the congregation, as well as what your (ideally) mutual aspirations are for what the congregation might yet become.

Upcoming programs. Here is your opportunity to talk about what new services and programs you hope to offer in the next year, five years, or ten years. Explain why these programs will help achieve your vision. And don't forget to explain who would benefit from these programs.

Remember that a story is a story and not a list of statistics! People can look at a leave-behind brochure or website for the facts. You want to offer your passion, your excitement, and the reason for your involvement. If done correctly, you will evoke a similar reaction in the person who listens.

The Written Case Statement

The case for giving will be similar whether spoken or written, but the expected level of detail is vastly different. That is not to say that you should list every fact you have, but the information in the written case statement should include data points that support the reason someone should give her philanthropic dollars and why the congregation is a good investment. (Keep in mind that you are not competing for donations with other synagogues but with other philanthropic organizations.)

Remember who you are writing the case statement for. We will say this time and time again in this book: fundraising is about the donor. What interests the donor? What is his life stage? When does he usually come into the building? Are there special lectures or events he likes to attend? What areas of the website is he reading? If you cannot figure this out from your research, ask. But then you have to be prepared to quickly focus the conversation toward the portion of the case that he will most likely respond to.

You can create one document and circle aspects that you think would be of interest. Alternatively, you could write a general information piece with various inserts that highlight areas of interest; these, then, can be included on an as-needed basis. It depends on how much such flexibility will mean to your success.

Be sure to respond to the essence of the future solicitation: "Why now?" Creating a sense of urgency—if it is real—is a strong motivator. But patience may be even more important for the donor to make a good decision. Tax deductions are not the primary reason that someone gives $25,000—or even $500. Instead, December has become a time when donors are in the habit of giving—a time ripe with possibilities for synagogues.

What you might ask yourself is whether a gift at this time allows you to launch a program or stage an event that otherwise might not occur. Could you establish a matching-gift program that will increase the donor's gift? Or, might this family establish a match to influence other donors for the end-of-fiscal-year appeal in June? Consider what would help you get the gift with enough urgency that the donor feels she should give now.

Include a story. The emotion within the written case is what the donor will read and reread—and should not be the same story shared in person. The emotion may be touching, like a story about how Ben, age five, had his first experience with the Torah. Learning that he couldn't use his hands to follow the words, he created a *yad* at home out of respect for his favorite book. Or inspirational, like the story of Naomi, who took an adult b'nai mitzvah class that eased her way into Torah learning and prompted her to attend the daily minyan. Maybe it is one that tugs on your heartstrings. After Karen's father died, she received such amazing support from the congregation that she started participating in synagogue life on a regular basis.

The stories should be real, ideally with names attached. This is not to cause embarrassment but instead to let prospective donors know that the synagogue is enhancing the lives of their friends, their neighbors, or the person they sat behind at services last week. Your congregation has a tangible impact on people's lives, and their donation could help sustain and promote more relationships, strengthen the community, offer additional learning opportunities, or even subsidize fees to encourage additional participation in youth activities.

Each story is one among the many in the congregation that makes you proud to be affiliated.

Staying Positive: Scaring Donors Only Makes Donors Scarce

You will not raise money out of desperation. We cannot say this enough. Your failure to raise enough money, forcing you to reach into the principal of your endowment for the past few years, does not give donors confidence that you will act responsibly with *their* money.

You might say, "But we had to do that because the community doesn't give enough each year." That may be the case (of course, that may have more to do with the fundraising plan than the donors), but that is not the way to fundraise. No one wants to give to a sinking ship. They want to jump onboard the boat that is cruising at full speed toward a mutually agreed–upon destination (like extra music study classes with the cantor) while fully supporting the rest of the programming. Would you give to an organization that told you your help would allow them to decrease the amount they will take from the endowment from $300,000 to $250,000? If they are still taking $250,000 each year, their survival is not guaranteed once the endowment runs out. Then your $50,000 was wasted.

If you say, "Yes, I will work harder to reach out to more donors, more times throughout the year with updates, reports on new developments, and other stewardship opportunities," then you are on the right track. Follow that up with a thought like this: "This year we are doing things differently. We are creating 'campaigns of one' for each donor with more data, more focus, and more one-on-one solicitations." And if that is truly the case, the donors will feel the difference right away. They will feel that they are giving to something that is growing in exciting ways that will support this vibrant community. The enthusiasm will be palpable and the gifts will be easier to get.

Worrying donors means that donors are worried about the state of your congregation. And worried donors who have heard this story from you more than once will translate the second and third cry for help as proof that you do not have a solid, long-term strategy in place. And that will only end in decreased funding from all but a few die-hard supporters.

Positive Messaging

Think about how you communicate your new outlook on every occasion. Talking about achievements helps donors see your strengths. Talk about your impact and your enthusiasm will shine through, even in tough times. And focus on what the donors will experience. Talk about the increased programmatic opportunities, not the needs of the executive director and the staff.

Focus on the new film and lecture series that you offered this year and explain how continuing that series requires stable funding for that and all the other programs the community values.

Or explain how the previous economic downturn had forced the reduction of two programs that you would like to bring back with the help of donors like them.

It is not that you do not have a need, it's just that you are not desperate or needy. And say it with a smile. Because scaring donors only makes donors scarce.

Why Too Many Details Can Do Your Synagogue Harm

There is often a reference to the iceberg metaphor in fundraising. There is a relatively small portion of what the synagogue offers that will appeal to any one donor. Donors want to know there is a lot more beneath the surface supporting the piece that they find appealing and beautiful.

And the good news is, the iceberg can be personalized for each donor, with the beneath-the-surface information available upon request. What icebergs should you consider?

- Post–b'nai mitzvah youth programming
- Updates to the chapel
- Senior-friendly learning opportunities
- Community Shabbat dinners
- A second-night seder
- Strengthening the office staff to support the current needs

You might want to highlight a couple of icebergs, but if you show donors a list of everything you want to support in the coming year, nothing will stick out (bad pun, but true). Too much information is overwhelming.

Instead, consider that you are offering curated content. If you frequent any websites with blogs, you will know that from your initial article you can click on some link that will take you to similar content. A food blog will include links to restaurants or recipes that include chicken. A nonprofit fundraising and development blog (like www.merskyjaffe.com) will allow you to focus on individual topics, such as board development or executive search, by clicking on the cloud tag. (We fully acknowledge this as a bit of self-promotion, but it *is* our book.)

People have now become accustomed to finding the information that is relevant to them while easily bypassing everything else. Give the people what they want. Cases for giving, as well as every other aspect of fundraising, should be about the prospect and her interests, not what the development director is most proud of achieving or the rabbi's favorite program.

Add Programs Judiciously

A donor tells you he is happy to give $20,000 to the annual fund to initiate a Torah study program at a nearby senior facility. Twenty thousand dollars is a lot of money. That could ease your shortfall substantially this year. Before you jump at the opportunity, consider:

- The costs of the program. Will $20,000 cover the costs of the clergy time, the staff time needed to make the arrangements, the marketing efforts necessary to encourage participation, the additional large-print books, as well as any other overhead that needs to be allocated to the project? A $20,000 program that costs $20,000, including allocated costs, will not alleviate your budgetary shortfall.
- Whether this is a program you had been seeking to offer. If you had been considering how to further your outreach in the community, this is a perfect opportunity to do so in a fully funded manner. If you do a lot of senior learning on site, and were hoping to expand the offerings this year for the empty nesters, then this might be a natural extension of that program. But if you do not have the capacity to launch an off-site initiative, the restricted $20,000 might cause more trouble than it is worth.

Before you say, "No, thank you," have a conversation with the donor to determine if he will consider donating that $20,000 to the general fund. A donor is offering a specific gift, but you can respond with something besides yes or no. You can ask if you could use the money toward supporting the current programming for seniors, including X, Y, and Z. Be honest and explain that taking on this new program right now would prevent you from fully supporting other projects that are already under way, and that you would never want to take on a new program unless you could do it well.

He might be disappointed, but if he is a supporter of the congregation as a whole, he will appreciate that you know your capacity limits and that you are looking at the budget holistically and thoughtfully. Getting back to our metaphor, a synagogue does not want to be seen as a bunch of ice floes created to satisfy donors without a solid foundation.

Chapter 10

The Effective Annual Fund

Not Just on Yom Kippur Anymore

Judaism is about tradition. So much so that Jews are willing to follow rules created centuries ago in a very different world. But these traditions remind us that we are a people chosen by God, that we are different and proud of it.

Then there is the tradition of the Yom Kippur appeal. It was not handed down with the Torah. It was not detailed by Maimonides or prescribed in the Talmud. It was not even deemed an essential part of the holiest of days, until synagogues realized that the High Holidays were the days that brought out the largest number of members who can be solicited all at once through one speech. And that encouraging the mitzvah of *tzedakah*—one of the big three that "averts the evil decree" as the gates are closing—might be a good incentive for the attendees.

Maybe you remember when the method to acknowledge the speech and the congregation's needs was a card you found on the seat when you walked in. Bending the appropriate tab denoted how much you were willing to give. And it worked. At least it worked for a while.

Then there was a revolutionary idea! What if we sent out a letter with the appeal *before* the speech, and then congregants didn't have to respond on site but at their leisure? Without the peer pressure of seeing everyone else handing in their tabbed cards, and with other nonprofits—Jewish and non-Jewish—working harder to get philanthropic dollars, things began to go downhill financially for many congregations.

People weren't responding. Another new idea surfaced! There needed to be follow-up! Communities started to include a personal call or a personalized note to the previous donors and, oftentimes, synagogues could convince enough people to contribute that they reached their goal.

Soon, even that wasn't enough. The fundraising industry, which kept coming up with ideas to improve synagogue bottom lines, helped increase fundraising for millions of nonprofits that are competing for those same dollars. The mitzvah of *tzedakah* could be fulfilled by giving to other organizations that attracted people's attention. And the feeling that Jews should support synagogues because that was what they were supposed to do was not a strong enough motivation.

So what went wrong? Other nonprofits started caring about their donors, while at the synagogue there was not enough stewardship to encourage giving. There was the once-a-year pitch with some follow-up asks instead of a year-round approach. Members may give something, but they are not going to give even close to their capacity with this kind of synagogue fundraising. Other nonprofits have become extremely good at creating the relationships that encourage donors, while synagogues are stuck in the 1950s.

The Yom Kippur appeal may be one component of a development program. But in order to change to a donor-centric approach, consider how the donor would like to give, with multiple giving opportunities at different times throughout the year, stewardship "touches," and dedication to the process. It is a lot more work for the staff and volunteer leadership. But it also has the potential to yield exponentially greater outcomes.

Overall Jewish Giving or Giving to Your Congregation?

One consideration when you determine what your case for giving should be is whether your prospects will be supporting being Jewish or supporting your congregational community. In days gone by, saying that your synagogue needed funding might have been enough to garner support from everyone affiliated, but those days are long gone. There are myriad local, national, and international nonprofits looking to compete with your synagogue.

What constitutes Jewish giving? Contributions to an organization with the word *Jewish* or *Israel* in its name? Or, is it any contribution made by a Jew and influenced by core Jewish values, such as *tikkun olam*, social justice, education, preservation of the environment, and the like?

Whatever definition you prefer, it is clear that Jews are by nature and tradition very generous. We give as a people. But our donations do not always go to Jewish causes, in general, or the synagogue, in particular, as demonstrated in two different studies from the Cohen Center for Modern Jewish Studies at Brandeis University, one a demographic study of a Midwestern community that showed that, while 92 percent of all Jews claimed to give philanthropically, less than 59 percent of the money went to Jewish causes. Fewer than 2 percent of the population made gifts of $5,000 or more to philanthropies—Jewish or non-Jewish. The other, a study of gifts of more than $1 million, found that 91 percent went to causes other than Jewish. And, with some very notable exceptions, the synagogue was rarely, if ever, the recipient of the most generous support of its members.

It's time to take a look at your donor strategy. What does it say about the cause and what does it say about the organization? You are an institution that teaches, supports, and promotes Judaism. But what makes your culture unique? If someone were "shul shopping" and asked a member why she belongs to this congregation, you want the answer to be easy to identify. And more substantial than that the rabbi is smart or that it is a one-shul town.

Do you promote social justice in general, and then help members take part in making changes? Are you inclusive and welcoming to all? Are there special groups to encourage involvement in the synagogue for unattached Millennials, those in Generations X and Y, or baby boomers (not as a way to meet potential partners but as a way to meet like-minded people)? Do you have a successful post–b'nai mitzvah teen group that encourages this contingent to stay involved? These are the programs that your community will support, not just because you are Jewish but because you are showing how Jewish values can positively impact your congregational community.

Creating a Strategy

Your strategy should be defined in the fundraising plan we presented in chapter 3. Now let's look at the specifics that will allow you to assess what you are currently doing to achieve your goals, what you want to do, and how you plan to get there—with specifics.

Organizational Objectives

Do you know where you have been and where you currently are, in terms of both your budget and your actual fundraising income? Consider this chart:

Fundraising Revenue by Source: Budget versus Actual

Fundraising Sources*	2016 Actual	2017 Budget	2017 Actual	+/– 2017 versus 2016
Yom Kippur appeal				
Gala				
Memorial gifts				
Endowment income				
Foundation support				
Other _____				
Other _____				
Total				

*The Fundraising Sources column intentionally ignores particular areas of income, like dues, High Holiday tickets, or preschool income, as those will not be a part of the fundraising plan.

Let's turn to the qualitative objectives. What are you hoping the synagogue will be able to achieve when you secure more funds? How will the synagogue feel different to members? To the community at large? To the other religious institutions around you? Specifying your intentions will allow others to see your vision for the potential of the community with more annual funding.

Writing and Implementing the Fundraising Plan

So who should write this plan? Should it be one person or a committee? This involves high-level strategizing for your synagogue, so it should be a priority for the senior development staff, if you have someone you consider senior. If not, the executive director should help develop the plan, potentially with the help of a few select board members. In other words, staff should be included, as they will have to say whether or not the goals are realistic from a practical standpoint. Those involved should understand:

- What you are currently doing
- Best industry practices that should be incorporated into the plan
- Your goals
- Your current infrastructure and what will potentially need an upgrade
- What it means to have vision beyond a budget that has a surplus

The Basic Structure

A fundraising plan is the overview of qualitative and quantitative current realities and goals, and the outline you will use to reach those goals. What should you include in your plan?

Fundraising Goals

In chapter 3, we recommended focusing on one or two specific goals (see page 23). Now it is time to choose those one or two key goals. Your plan should include a financial target of how much money you seek to raise, as well as the number of donors by dollar range it will take to achieve success. Part of any good annual campaign is to have a broad base of support, representative of the community as a whole. No campaign can be truly successful if there are only a handful of donors. While it is true that a small number of donors will provide the bulk of the financial goal (the infamous 80/20 rule), you want to amass an army of contributors to achieve a true sense of community support.

The financial goal should be rooted in reality. Understand your current budget as well as projections of requirements for the coming year. Don't increase next year's budgeted revenue by 20 percent just so you have a little room to breathe, unless you can show that 20 percent is necessary right now. That is not to say that you cannot increase your goals. Consider how you will justify any increases. People will ask for an explanation and you will be expected to respond thoughtfully and responsibly. And saying, "We just want to have extra money so we can do more" is not going to prompt donors to offer additional funds.

Strategies and Tactics

This is where you explain how you will achieve your goals. For instance, in terms of overall direction, this year we will focus on gaining new donors of $250 or more, while we seek to retain 80 percent of all prior donors of $250 or more. Why? When we examined our current membership, only 43 percent gave to the annual fund last year. While they are essential to funding our congregation, we would like to increase the number of new or first-time donors—as well as revived PYBUNTS—to realize a 51 percent rate of participation.

Be specific and list your tactics. For example, we will retain donors by:

- Utilizing new donor software that strengthens our donor tracking and points out trends in our congregation.
- Using prospect research to identify current donors with increased philanthropic capacity in our community.
- Creating individual strategies to encourage giving from this group of prospects and create "campaigns of one" (see page 4).
- Making every gift above $X,XXX a face-to-face solicitation.
- Encouraging increased donations from everyone by personalizing past giving history and asking for 125–150 percent of last year's gift in the appeal letter.
- Adding an email thank-you note to all donors from the office. This will be in addition to the formal printed thank-you that is signed by the board member and the formal tax receipt sent by the office at the end of year. This is simply an acknowledgment of the gift.
- Adding three follow-up emails during November and December to encourage donors to give before the end of the calendar year.
- Establishing an annual regular monthly thank-a-thon, where board members call donors who gave in the previous thirty days to thank them for their support.
- Listing donors who have given for more than ten consecutive years in the synagogue newsletter and on the website's fundraising page (and potentially separating out those who have given for more than twenty-five or fifty years).

- Continuing the annual donor event, but this year send out a survey to see if a different day of the week or time would work better for the majority of attendees.
- Considering other ways to "touch" and steward donors.
- Continuing the Yom Kippur appeal, gala, and foundation requests. In addition, we will begin to accept donations online. We have been reluctant to do this, due to credit card fees, but we keep hearing that donors will give more and more easily through an online option.

We will attract new donors by:

- Seeking a challenge grant to double any member's first-time gift this year during our April appeal.
- Using prospect research to identify new donor prospects with substantial giving capacity in our community.
- Creating individual strategies to encourage giving from this group of prospects.
- Sponsoring five gateway events this year (see chapter 16).
- Assigning board or development committee members to meet with prospects and answer any potential questions about the annual fund.
- Creating a leave-behind that explains the benefits of the annual fund.
- Offering a "new donor" brunch with the clergy.

The plan will assign goals, costs, and administrative responsibilities to each new element of your strategy: additional letters, emails, personal solicitations, special events, and phonathons. Staff time should be considered as well. Do you currently have the capacity or will you need additional staff or consulting resources to incorporate these ideas? If the staff cannot take on these new responsibilities, who will make sure it happens in a timely fashion? Only take on what you can handle until you expand the support staff, but don't hold off until you can easily afford the support staff. It may be the classic chicken-and-egg question, but there is no doubt who loses when indecision causes a lack of forward movement.

PART IV

Why It's Okay to Ask for a Donation

Chapter 11

Creating a Culture of Asking

What is a "culture of asking"? This term refers to shifting the culture of a synagogue, or any nonprofit, to a place that is unafraid to solicit donations. An organization with a culture of asking is willing to research, cultivate, and solicit donors; has strong leadership with vision, whose volunteer leaders and staff are open to trying new things; and establishes itself as an organization that directly asks its members for funding.

Personal Solicitations

Who should be asked? Everyone. Starting with the board, followed by the committees, and, last but not least, each member of the congregation. By eliminating any members from the list of those you solicit, you are taking away the opportunity for them to feel good about their impact on the congregation. Even if they are on reduced dues, they should have the opportunity to give to the annual fund.

Defining a Personal Solicitation

A personal solicitation is not a personalized letter. It is not a personalized email. It is not a follow-up phone call. It is a face-to-face meeting. It is an interactive conversation that creates a relationship between the prospective donor and the synagogue. It offers the prospect the chance to voice an opinion and it offers the solicitor the opportunity to ask for a gift in person. Your success with letters and emails will pale in comparison to your success in face-to-face meetings.

Who should be asked via a personal solicitation? It is unfortunate that you cannot approach every donor and prospect personally. Is there an internal designation for a "major gift"? If so, that is where you could make your cutoff. If you are lucky, you will have to set up one hundred meetings. But, if you have only been sending out letters and emails for years, you are more likely to have twenty-five to fifty beyond the board.

Who Should Solicit These Gifts?

Since you should always start with board gifts (see page 49), the obvious place to start is with board members soliciting other board members. Have the board chair ask the group who is comfortable soliciting their fellow board members.

> Note: The first year will be a bit harder than years to follow. You are encouraging a move outside their comfort zone, but in just a few short years this will become the way your board works.

Assuming that less than a quarter of the board will volunteer, you will then ask each volunteer to solicit three or four other board members. These conversations are an ideal time to practice solicitation skills. You are asking people you know, who will give at some level, to join you in donating to a place you both care about. Solicitations don't get much easier than that.

While you want to develop a strategy for each donor (see chapter 12 for more details), board members often have suggested minimum donations. These are only the starting point, not the ultimate ideal donation for each member. In other words, do not let minimum expected gifts become maximums.

If you know from your research that Lynn gives other organizations $10,000, but only gives the board minimum of $2,500 to the congregation, ask if she will consider increasing her gift to $5,000 this year. Don't say no for her. She has her own voice to say yes or no, and will not give more out of guilt. She may give more because she believes in the community and all that you do.

Once the board solicitations are done, ask if any additional board members are now willing to widen the circle by asking committee members and major givers for a gift. You may find that once they have given their personal gift, they are willing to join in solicitations.

What If the Board President Is Reluctant to Do Fundraising?

Ideally, board presidents are natural fundraisers. In practice, they may have other skills that helped them land this leadership role. Have a solicitor who's comfortable with fundraising accompany the board president, but do not allow the president to avoid fundraising. If he is not invested in the process, he will not help you raise more money. And if there is not enough support from the top, it will be that much harder to achieve your new goals.

Reduced Dues

It feels counterintuitive to ask someone for money who is getting a scholarship, but it shouldn't be. The first step is to change your mentality.

You might be thinking along these lines: "How can they give anything? If they had an extra $18, shouldn't they have added that to their dues?" If so, you are being unfair and judgmental about the way they spend their money.

For people on a limited income, you are reducing their dues because their relationship with the synagogue is not transactional, but based on a relationship. You want them as a part of the community. You want them to feel that you value them as members. Their gift to the annual fund will allow them to fully participate in synagogue life, including donor events. And once you have agreed to reduce their dues, it is not up to you to determine how they spend the rest of their money.

You may be thinking something else, like this: "What about those families who don't really need a dues reduction but get one anyway? Then they get to give to the annual fund and feel good about how generous they are?" That line of thinking is ungenerous. People ask for a dues abatement for a variety of reasons. Even if you know they take three vacations a year and have good incomes, you have a choice as to whether you abate their dues or not. Again, how they spend the rest of their money is not up to you. You do not get to judge them because you have intimate knowledge of their financial relationship with the synagogue.

Instead, consider that, in all likelihood, they are paying the amount for dues that they feel their membership is worth. If they give to the annual fund, it may be because they feel able to give a onetime gift but are hesitant to alter their modified dues status for future years. Or, they are offering a larger family gift. Or, they have a company match that they want to use to support the congregation in a way that they cannot do on their own. Or any number of reasons that you are not privy to. The thing is that you can spend a lot of energy being angry about something or you can just be gracious and take the high road. The high road always offers a much more peaceful view.

Generosity Exemplified

An eastern, urban congregation with which we are familiar helps their large number of elderly members on fixed incomes donate to a variety of funds—including the annual fund—each year. At the start of their congregation's year, they ask those on fixed incomes or in need of reduced dues to offer the amount they feel comfortable giving to the synagogue this year—in total. Maybe it is $100; maybe it is more. But each person in need of abatement determines her own total. In the $100 example, half is put toward her dues. The other $50 is held in reserve in case she wants to give in honor of a *simcha*, honor someone who has died, or, you guessed it, contribute to the annual fund.

The generosity of this policy does not change this congregation's total revenue; it simply alters the buckets the funds are going into. It may cause more paperwork, but can you imagine how different it feels to these members? That satisfied feeling you get when you believe you helped the shul you care about is what you want to give each and every member of your congregation.

One Hundred Percent Board Participation Is Essential

Let's make this clear and straightforward. You will not reach your full potential unless you have 100 percent board participation for your annual fund. To put it bluntly, if each member of the board does not support the annual fund, why should anyone else?

The board is the congregational leadership. Board members should be leading the way in making exemplary donations to the annual fund.

Board members help determine how funds are spent. So they should set the example by contributing to those funds.

The board determines the vision for the congregation. If board members are not helping make that vision a reality with their financial commitment, then they are impeding its progress.

Participation also allows 100 percent of board members to help with fundraising. Whether they are soliciting gifts or making thank-you calls, the conversation can be focused on the community they are supporting. "I hope you will join me in helping Congregation Emanuel become the best we can be." "Thank you for joining me in helping Congregation Emanuel be the best we can be."

One hundred percent board participation shows that the board is willing to put their money where their mouth is. They are not asking someone to do anything they wouldn't do. The amounts may differ, but as long as they are all meaningful gifts (see page 123), they are fulfilling one of the essential fiduciary responsibilities of a board member.

How to Ask Your Friends and Neighbors for Support

Did you know there is a magic trick to asking your friends and neighbors for support? People who have solicited someone they know understands the magic. And anyone who doubts that the secret could be so simple has never made this type of solicitation.

So what is the secret?

You ask. You call a prospect and set up a meeting, ideally at his home. You work with the development committee leadership to find out everything you can about his giving history, current circumstances, and any other prospect research. You determine the amount you think will create the best balance of feeling good about giving and knowing the organization can use that money to strengthen the amazing congregational experience. And you ask.

Refer to chapter 13 for details on what should go into the ask, but keep in mind that if you don't ask, you will not receive. And if you do receive a gift, it will not be close to his capacity 95 percent of the time (this number is based on our experience only). And if you are willing to accept an easy gift, rather than asking someone for a specific increased gift, you should not expect any increases in your fundraising numbers. You might as well close this book and pass it along to the friend you are not willing to solicit. But don't blame us when she solicits you.

Calling a friend is not as hard as you would think. Presumably, the friend knows you are intimately involved with the congregation's board. When you call and say that you are calling on behalf of Congregation Emanuel, your friend will probably laugh and ask if you are calling to solicit her. You can offer one of a few responses:

- Congregation Emanuel has asked me to start solicitations and I can really use some practice. Do you think I could talk to you about the exciting programs we are developing and get some feedback on how you think we are doing as a temple, as well as how I am doing explaining it all?
- A solicitation can only happen after I talk to you about some of the new programs we are developing at Congregation Emanuel. Can I come over and talk to you and David about all the exciting programs?
- Before I can solicit you, I want to set up a time with you to talk about the exciting programs we are developing at Congregation Emanuel. I think some of them will really interest you and we are looking for feedback on where we are heading.
- I know you have been concerned about the direction of the congregation in the past couple of years. Do you think I could come over and talk to you about it in an informal way so that I can report back to the rest of the leadership? If I happen to solicit you, it will only be because you agree that Congregation Emanuel is in such a terrific place.

Do you see the trend? You are not trying to fool this prospect. Soliciting gifts should always include updates and opportunities for feedback. You are offering them the ears of the leadership. And with a well-prepared solicitation strategy, you know how to walk them step-by-step through the process and achieve your goals.

What If They Say No?

Remember not to take it personally—or let it affect your friendship. Make it clear that you are asking him because you are his friend. And make sure you mean that.

He can say no, and while you may try to convince him otherwise, you want him to give because he also wants to support the synagogue.

Gifts should feel good to give—not as if you are twisting someone's arm or asking for his last bit of disposable income. If he is feeling as if that is the case, you should review your techniques. If you have not been overly aggressive, then he is probably reacting to past solicitations. You may offer to sit and listen to his concerns and promise no ask. It may not mean a gift this year, but it will mean a more satisfied congregant. And that should always be a priority.

We're All in This Together

Some find it awkward or feel it is an imposition to ask a fellow congregant for money. That is often caused by the idea that the act of asking creates an uneven power balance between fellow congregants or friends. This is understandable when you consider that whoever is asking may know inside information about the prospect's situation, or the fact that this person is in temple leadership and the prospect is not. The outsider often feels slightly intimidated by the insider. Just ask any high school student.

But we are not high school students. And you, as a solicitor, are not profiting from the results of the annual fund any more than any other congregant. A solicitor does not automatically get access to the clergy, a better seat at the Torah study group, or first chance to sign up for an exciting lecture. The whole congregation benefits by financial sustainability, the opportunity to create new programs, and the appropriate building maintenance.

Fundraising success and life itself are altered by your perspective on the situation. You can choose to look at a solicitation as an imposition or you can choose to look at it as an opportunity. If you can't get past the discomfort you may initially feel, you will never be successful in soliciting gifts. And, while you may still believe in the project, it might be best to be honest with everyone and offer to help with prospect research or join in others' solicitations to provide support—and leave the asks to others.

Chapter 12

Basic Fundraising Skills

A Strategy for Each Donor

What does it mean to have a strategy for each donor? Let's say you have five hundred member units. That means you have five hundred individuals or families you should consider as prospects. As we have mentioned before, you are trying to get as close to 100 percent participation as possible, but not every synagogue will have a complicated, multistep strategy with one-on-one meetings. So let's consider how to allocate your time.

Step 1: Segment your existing donor database and select your best major gift prospects. Ideally, you will place them in one of four categories: A, B, C, or D.

- An "A" will be in the first tier or among the most likely prospects.
- A "B" will be in the second round of personal asks—people with unknown potential or a weaker connection to the synagogue.
- A "C" will be the group that this year will be asked through a personal letter with follow-up emails and phone calls.
- A "D" is the group you should not ask right now for some reason; for example, a member has asked not to be solicited or he is angry with the congregation. You don't want to simply remove people from the list, because it will be impossible to track what happened in the future.

Let's leave B and C aside for now and focus on the A's.

Step 2: Create a file for each prospective donor. In the old days, there was literally a file that held all the information on each person. Now there should be a file in your fundraising software for each person. Capabilities vary, but you should be able to track:

- Previous giving (amounts and years)
- What the person gave to or for (annual fund, events, support of a lecture series)
- The date of each gift
- How the gift arrived (in the mail, in person, or online)
- Any restrictions, contingencies, or guidelines that came with each gift
- Any interactions with the fundraising department worth noting
- Anything that might affect giving (happy about the new preschool director, dissatisfied with the way her friend was treated recently)

You will need a physical file to hold signed pledge forms, copies of checks, and any other physical documentation related to fundraising. Check with your congregation's accountants to find out what they require.

Step 3: Collect research. Prospect research is the only way that you will be able to uncover hidden jewels, understand true capacity, and know who should be in the first group (see chapter 8 for full details). If you base your research on the same data you have been using for years, you will end up with very similar results. Assuming that you are reading this book to improve your fundraising, using old research will be wasting everyone's time and energy.

Step 4: Identify and consult with natural partners. Volunteers can help in developing relationships with each prospect. The donor who appears on paper to be able to give large amounts is worth, well, the cost of the paper if he has no strong connection to the synagogue.

Find out whether a board or committee member currently has a relationship with the individual or family. If no one springs to mind, consider who could naturally form a relationship. Of course, this is not just about fundraising. You have just identified a congregant who does not have a strong connection to the synagogue. The idea that you will, at some point, ask her for financial support is only part of the story. As it should be.

Step 5: Develop a strategy and gift objectives for each prospect. Each congregation has a different threshold for what is considered a major gift, which means each congregation must determine who should receive a one-on-one solicitation, who is ready to have a conversation about her gift, and who has the potential to make a larger gift this year.

It's not as hard as it sounds. Create an Excel spreadsheet with all five hundred names. Print out one copy for each committee member and collate the list by page number. It will be approximately twelve pages long. Then hand out one copy of the first page to each committee member and ask everyone to rate the prospects in one of four categories:

A. Has the capacity and likelihood to give a major gift this year. There is potential to increase the gift. The natural partner is obvious and the family feels a strong connection to the synagogue.

B. Either has the capacity but is missing the connection or might have the capacity (research isn't always clear-cut) and needs to be explored, but has the potential to be a major donor.

C. May have a strong giving history and a strong connection, but does not have the financial resources to make a major gift. These people should be recognized if they are consistent supporters, but will not receive face-to-face solicitations.

D. Everyone else who will not be solicited. This category will be a potpourri of people who have showed some sign that a solicitation—even via a letter—will cause ire. This is the category of people who need to see a different side of the synagogue or its development committee before they can be solicited. This group should be tracked and considered at less busy times of the year.

Collect the information and create an official rating for each member. Then re-sort the list by letter, printing out A's in preparation for the next committee meeting. Do this for all the pages in the document, working your way through the list one meeting at a time.

Step 6: Create a "campaign of one" plan that lists the next five moves for each prospect. For each person or family, you should determine the five steps that will move you toward your goals of deeper engagement and larger donations. What kind of moves would be appropriate for each prospect?

- Invitations to events—is there something that would be of interest in the near future?
- One-on-one encounters.
- Email updates—individual (if so, from whom and on what topic) or group (again, from whom and on what topic).
- Letters—personal or the appeal letter? Will there be a handwritten note?
- Newsletter or newspaper articles that would be of interest.
- Phone calls to check in or provide answers to questions the prospect raised.

Remember that you are trying to "move" them toward their next (or first) gift, which means deepening their relationship. (Moves will be discussed in chapter 15.)

Before you default to your annual appeal letter as your first point of contact, remember that you are trying to make a change. Will doing the same thing that you have been doing for ten years or more encourage a different response from prospects? Of course not! It's time to shake things up for you and for them.

Step 7: Modify the plan as necessary. This plan is not static, but dynamic. Change it as circumstances and new information warrant.

This is a lot of work—no question—but you are looking for a substantial change. And substantial changes require effort in every aspect of life. Just keep in mind the end goal of creating a stronger annual fund, which will enable you to achieve more!

Getting Organized Before the Ask

More than half the success in the engagement and solicitation of a funder is achieved before you meet with a prospect. The ask should be the culmination of extensive research of and conversations about the donor. This may be a few days' work or the product of several years of research, but the methodology that you follow to ensure success is the same. Keeping all the information you gather organized and retrievable is vital.

Gathering Information

Prospect and donor management fundraising software has limitations—with the possible exception of a fully customizable, flexible solution. (If you are using member management software as fundraising software, there are even more limitations.) It's the nature of creating one solution for many synagogues; the one feature that seems obvious to one development committee is irrelevant to others.

What do you want to track consistently?

- Which prospects are assigned to each solicitor.
- How far along each solicitor is in his approach to each potential donor.
- The amount you expect to receive from each donor.
- The percentage of that amount that was brought in (by individual solicitors and the solicitation team as a whole).
- Donors who will only make verbal pledges as opposed to those who have confirmed their commitments in writing.
- How often each donor has been contacted about her pledge.
- Who, within your congregation and office, is responsible for each point of contact with each donor (that is, calls, thank-you letters, sending pledge reminders, and the like).
- Participation levels for each constituent group (board members, parents, alumni by class) associated with the congregation.

We could go on, but just as no software is one-size-fits-all, our list cannot be all-encompassing for everyone reading this book. But software, even used to its fullest potential, cannot be the only thing you rely on.

The important thing to remember is to know what you are tracking, why you are tracking it, and who should have access to this data. Then you can consider which specific software to acquire, such as Excel spreadsheets, Google Docs, Dropbox, or Microsoft SharePoint. It may seem as if you need a list of lists. Annoying? Perhaps. Essential? Definitely.

Letters Can Be Effective

While the entire annual appeal strategy should not be based on a letter sent to congregants, letters may still be effective. And enough research has been done in the field that there are ways to make your letter more effective.

First, let's consider segmentation of your donor list. If you have a strategy for each donor and fundraising software that will allow you to sort and re-sort based on giving history, consider incorporating the following categories:

- Donors who gave last year. This can also be broken down as follows:
  - Donors who gave for the first time last year
  - Donors who have given for more than five, ten, or twenty-plus years
  - Donors who gave more than one time in the year
  - Donors whose gift last year was their highest gift ever
  - Donors who increased their gift last year over the previous year
- Donors who gave in the past few years, but not last year. This can also be broken down as follows:
  - Those who didn't give in the last fiscal year, but did give in the previous fiscal year
  - Those who didn't give in the last two fiscal years, but gave some years before that
  - Those who didn't give in the last fiscal year, but gave before some major change in the organization (such as a new rabbi or executive director, a new focus, a board shift, and the like)
- Prospective donors, also known as "never-evers." This can also be broken down as follows:
  - Prospects who have potential to be major donors
  - Prospects of more modest means
  - Prospects who are new to the community

You do not need to add in each category, but you should consider which categories are represented in your list and which would help you talk more directly to your donors or prospects.

That is the true purpose of segmentation—to connect with the donor on as personal a level as possible. The more generic a letter, the more likely it will end up in the recycling bin—if donors even open the mail that comes from the congregation. And that is a waste of everyone's time and energy.

The Eight-Plus Letter Essentials

1. *Personalization.* Each letter should include a personalized name, an inclusive feel using pronouns like *you* and *I*, and a specific ask amount. This is no longer a nice option; it is expected.
2. *The story.* What impression do you want the reader to take away from this letter? Consider which of the following stories has a greater impact.
    - We are proud that our congregation is making a difference in the lives of our members and the Jewish community as a whole.
    - Liz Karten is going to college next year and wondering if she will ever find a group that can replicate her Congregation Emanuel friends. Starting as preschool playmates, they have continued to form her Jewish community through high school.
3. *Tone.* Keep the tone consistent. The tone of the letter, just as in all writing, conveys an impression as much as the content. It should sound like it comes from one heartfelt voice, not a composite of editors, making it read more like a corporate image brochure than anything else.
4. *The asks.* Not just one—there should be multiple asks in each letter. Current theories lean toward three. One in the first paragraph or two. One toward the signature, and one in the postscript. It sounds like a lot, but every time you receive a solicitation from a national or international nonprofit you can see how it's done. Does the letter sound too forward? That's okay—you're asking for money!
5. *Length.* We advocate that letters to a congregational community should be a single page. You do not have to explain your mission or vision in this letter. You don't have to introduce new concepts. You can simply hit the important points, offer a story, and ask for a gift.

    While some people will read every letter, most people will skim it at best. They know why you are writing them at a certain time of year. The goal is to give them a reason to say "I want to give" not "I'll have to read through this and decide if we should give this year. I'll just put it in the pile with the fifty other letters I recently received."

6. *Focus.* Is the letter about the organization or about the prospect? It's sometimes tricky to get the balance right, but the letter should be about how the prospect will benefit from the synagogue, not how the synagogue will benefit from the donor's gift. Consider this excerpt from an appeal letter:

> If your circumstances drastically changed and membership at the temple became a hardship, would we ever turn you away?
>
> Of course not, because we support our community through good times and bad. Your contributions ensure that we can afford to make everyone feel welcome.
>
> You are helping our congregation support those in need, but you're also subsidizing the Hebrew school so that financial concerns are never the reason a child misses out on a Jewish education.

There is no doubt that the congregation as a whole will benefit from the support, but the donor has now put himself in the situation before offering a response.

7. *The reply mechanism.* Is there an envelope? A tear-off option? A web address? Does it invite you to give today? Or does it invite you to join the community that supports Jewish experiences at every life cycle stage? Every letter on the page is a way to shift the prospect's perspective on giving to your congregation this year. And while you might not like online giving due to credit card fees, it's not about you—it's about the donor. If she wants to give via credit card because it's easier, because she wants to earn credit card points, or because she wants easy tracking of her gifts on a credit card statement, she wants to give to you and you should make it as easy as possible!

8. *Editing.* One person writes a letter and two or three people edit it. Does this sound familiar? Editors should keep a few essentials in mind:

   - It may not reflect your tone, but unless your name is on it, only make grammatical changes or content changes, not changes in tone or style. However, if you think the whole letter is stylistically wrong for the congregation, you should definitely speak up.
   - Do not change the format based on the way you like to write. Certain aspects of appeal letters improve response rates—the

postscript, bullets, boldface type, and highlights. Even if your name is on it, everyone knows it is an appeal letter and will have a structure different from that of a personal letter.

- Do not think that you are a better writer or editor than every-one else. That assumption alone will give you the "authority" to make changes because you "know" what is right. Writing is not that cut-and-dried, language is often used (and misused) to achieve certain goals, and just because you like or dislike a particular section does not make it right or wrong.
- More writing does not equal more money. More writing will, in all likelihood, mean that less of the letter is read. Stick to the essentials and one good story. Save the rest for other points of contact.

Are You Following Up with Email?

Unless you're a member of Generation Y or a Millennial, email was not always in your life (and many Millennials skip email for texting and other forms of communication). It is considered both a convenience and an annoyance. It allows connection and conversation, but can feel overwhelming. And then there is all the spam.

However you feel, email is now a legitimate means of communica-tions for friends, family, businesses, and nonprofits alike. You may have a second email address for "junk" email, but the difference between email you want to read and junk blurs when your favorite store is offer-ing you 50 percent off. In other words, whether you like it or not, most of us rely on email much more than we would like.

We are not afraid to click DELETE; some of us do so judiciously and others with impunity, preferring an empty inbox. But none of us feels bad for a company or nonprofit when we click to delete a message. We may feel bad that we are not using the good deal from the Gap or not giving this year to Heifer International, but we probably feel good about ourselves at the moment we delete the message.

This is why you should not feel bad emailing follow-ups to snail-mailed solicitations as part of your overall strategy for all prospect categories. These emails can be personalized, provide specific asks, and highlight an additional aspect of your annual fund. They may get deleted, but they may get read. And online giving continues to increase exponentially each year.

If you are sure your friends don't give online, ask them. Choose five friends with similar demographics. Inquire whether they have given a gift online in the past year, whether the email they clicked on was the original request or simply served as a reminder for them to do it right then and there, and whether they noticed if there were other emails from the same nonprofit.

The truth is that nonprofits send out so many solicitations through email that it is often hard to remember what you have received from whom. What you do remember is which organizations you want to give to and whether it is easy to give.

Since the "campaign of one" is about the donor, not about that one board member who hates email, consider whether your donors want to be solicited in this manner or would prefer to opt out. If you are having a face-to-face meeting, you can simply ask or you can look at his history. Has he opted out of general mailings or does he tend to sign up for events through online newsletters? Has he given online in the past? Each of your members will give you clues as to their preferences. And if you are still not convinced, try a split-list test this year, sending out four follow-up emails to half of your list and one to the rest. Then you will know what works best for your members and know what to do in the future.

You have to consider what elements of social media will capture your younger prospects. And before you say, "Our congregation won't give that way," remember that you should never say no for a prospect or donor.

Yes, Larger Gifts Often Require More Work

It seems slightly unfair that just because someone has more money, she gets solicited for advice more often than someone with less financial potential. Life is unfair. The wealthy have advantages, but before you go off and rant about this, keep in mind a couple of other considerations:

- Nonprofits have to establish tiers of priorities to have someplace to start when soliciting gifts. It only makes sense to start with the largest donors.

- While a $50 donation may have a greater impact on one donor's financial situation than $50,000 on another's, $50,000 is not given out without careful consideration.
- The $50,000 gift probably started as a $1,000 or $2,500. A relationship needed to be nurtured until the donor understood the importance and impact of an increased gift.
- The best way to deepen the relationship with a donor is to ensure that the relationship goes beyond pure fundraising. This takes time and energy.
- Nonprofits have established premium giving levels that require more work—someone has to arrange the donor dinner with the speaker-in-residence.
- Once you offer premium thank-you gifts associated with giving levels, the expectations are that you will continue to offer these premiums.

Twenty-Two Common Fundraising Mistakes

When listing the twenty-two most common fundraising mistakes people are likely to make, it can sound as if there are too many pitfalls to avoid. Instead, consider these as simple strategies to keep in mind during your solicitations. You might even identify problems that you have had or of which you are afraid. Perhaps then you will be more successful when you are face-to-face with your next major gift prospect.

Mistake #1: Not maintaining a year-round focus. Maintain a commitment to results all year round. Fundraising should be a steady stream of encouraging new gifts and stewardship. If you only talk to prospects about fundraising in the fall, you are only talking to them when they are hearing from sixty other nonprofits soliciting them for gifts. Instead, consider your year-round strategy, using every tool at your disposal and implementing new ideas quickly.

Mistake #2: Not listening to the prospect. When you are with a prospect, never interrupt. Get the prospect to talk. Respond with key facts but do not immediately launch into the empathetic story that you think will make the connection. That story is too much about you. Instead, focus on his concerns, and send the right message, both verbally and nonverbally: "I am here to help you."

Mistake #3: Not empathizing with the prospect. While you don't want to tell a story to show empathy, you should have an understanding of the prospect's current circumstances. Always try to see the other person's perspective, remembering that you are not going to be the most important item on the day's agenda, even if she is the most important item on yours.

Mistake #4: Saying no for the donor. We cannot say this enough. You may think the gift is unlikely, but if you say no for the prospect, you are precluding the possibility. What if the prospect just wants to voice his concerns? Or maybe the prospect wants to give directed funds but never knew how. Or maybe, just maybe, his mind-set has changed since you last spoke with him and you are keeping him from helping the community.

Mistake #5: Seeing the prospect as an adversary. You have to strive to get the prospect to work with you; do not approach the meeting from a confrontational mind-set. The prospect should be considered an ally, someone you want on your team. This is someone you are encouraging to work with you to fulfill your mutual dreams for the synagogue.

Mistake #6: Getting distracted. Concentrate throughout your meeting, maintain eye contact, and do not get too far off topic with confusing or negative remarks. You want to address the issues, but not get dragged into the mire.

Mistake #7: Not taking notes. You can establish control of the meeting and reinforce the idea that you are there to share the prospect's thoughts with the entire leadership when you write them down. It is also easier to reconstruct a record of the meeting when you have your notes to refer to later.

Mistake #8: Failing to follow up. Thank-you notes, information the prospective donor expressed interest in, and responses to her concerns are essential points in the development cycle. Failing to follow up will leave the impression that you are not as responsible as she would like, and should not be trusted with a meaningful investment.

Mistake #9: Not keeping in contact with past donors. Remember that someone who has already given may be your best prospect for another—

and possibly increased—gift. It is always easier to retain a donor than to find a new donor.

Mistake #10: Assuming all donors are the same. We have talked about "campaigns of one" to focus on the differences between each prospect. Each prospect requires individual attention if you would like an individual gift.

Mistake #11: Not taking the prospect's point of view. When talking with the prospect, specify the benefits of making the gift not only for the congregation but also for the prospect. A donor-centric appeal shows that you understand why this gift would fit into the prospect's philanthropic priorities.

Mistake #12: Not taking pride in your work. You should stand behind your synagogue with pride. Talk frequently with others about what you do for the community. When you can no longer take pride in the relationship and your work, it is time to take a closer look at what is causing this lack of enthusiasm. Is the congregation changing? Are you? Are you satisfied with the direction of the change? Is it time for you to let others take over? If you do not live the dream, it will be hard to convince others to see it.

Mistake #13: Trying to convince, rather than convey. You can demonstrate in a compelling way how a gift can address the prospect's concerns. You should never apply high-pressure tactics that ignore the needs of the prospect.

Mistake #14: Underestimating the prospect's intelligence. No one wants a lecture on the amazing attributes of the synagogue. Lectures assume the prospect has a lack of knowledge and are a one-way conversation. Instead, work with the prospect to identify his interests and his understanding of the challenges you face, and work together to find solutions.

Mistake #15: Not keeping up-to-date. Do not assume that once a gift has closed you need no longer attempt to learn about the issues facing the donor. A donation should be the beginning of a long and mutually beneficial relationship.

Mistake #16: Rushing the "sale." Let the development cycle progress at the pace that's most appropriate for the prospect. Be patient. You will always do better by waiting for the prospect to be ready than by forcing a false (or even a real) sense of urgency on the solicitation. Your needs can be explained, but if the prospect is not ready, the prospect is not ready.

Mistake #17: Not using people proof. Build credibility by highlighting past successes with other donors. Solicitors should have all given their own gifts, so then you are asking the prospect to join you and the 102 other families that understand the importance of giving to the annual fund.

Mistake #18: Humbling yourself. Operate from the assumption that you bring to the table a specific set of skills and a level of knowledge from which the other person can benefit. Work with the prospect as a partner. The prospect's status as a philanthropist or high earner does not diminish who you are or make you any less valuable to the process.

Mistake #19: Taking rejection personally. Try to develop resilience and self-assurance when confronting rejection. Remember that hearing a no answer may be the only way to get to a yes answer. *No* often means, *No, not yet.*

Mistake #20: Not assuming responsibility. When faced with a no answer, consider asking the prospect where you have gone wrong, or what mistakes you might have made in the presentation. Even if the reason she is not giving is because the congregation is not her philanthropic priority, she might help you shape the presentation in a way that would highlight alternative aspects or a different way to approach the conversation for those less involved.

Mistake #21: Underestimating the importance of prospecting. Develop good prospecting skills, and work daily to find new donors. Adding new donors should always be a priority.

Mistake #22: Focusing on negatives. You should approach obstacles from a positive frame of mind. Avoid negative habits, such as complaining, and never, never gossip. Some prospective donors will try to find out insider information during these conversations, but always respect the community's privacy.

Chapter 13

The Individual Ask

Follow Up. Follow Up. Follow Up.

Why would we *start* a chapter with "Follow Up"? Because without a plan for following up, you will make your work 4½ times harder, since you will constantly be losing donors and having to search for new prospects. (It takes 4½ times the effort and dollars to *acquire* a new donor as it does to *keep* one, according to the Institute for Charitable Giving.) In a secular nonprofit, that is hard. In a congregational setting, you have a limited pool of prospects and you do not want to eliminate half of them because you do not have a disciplined system in place.

Donor follow-up can be planned at the same time the solicitation strategy is created. Follow-up does not have to be unique to the donor but it should be tailored to the situation. Ideas include:

- Email a thank-you for the meeting and/or the gift within twenty-four hours of the meeting. If you meet on a Friday and know that you will not email on Shabbat, send the email a few hours after the meeting. Acknowledge specific questions that you will need more time to answer and add that you look forward to continuing your conversation in the future.
- Share whether or not the conversation resulted in a gift. Send the information to the committee and/or staff (you will have previously set up who gets what information so that it is consistent for each case). This is both to share the news and to ensure the multiple ways of recognizing and acknowledging the gift start immediately. Will someone else want to make a call or write a personal note? Or have coffee to thank the donor for his donation? Should

he receive a gift acknowledgment form to ensure that he is listed properly on the website and in the newsletter?

- If there was no closure and a gift has not yet been secured, determine the next point of contact. Did you say you would call the prospect again soon? Was there interest expressed in sharing concerns with the clergy?
- Was there additional information that the prospect was promised or questions that needed to be answered? By whom? And how will the material be delivered?

Is Your Annual Appeal Follow-up Getting Through?

Raise your hand if you have a "dummy" email address for anything that you think might clutter your email inbox. Or anything you think you should sign up for but don't really want to see very often. A lot of people do this, but then no one wants to check these coupon-, discount-, and spam-laden accounts.

Are you ending up in the spam address? How can you ensure your annual appeal follow-up messages are getting through? Or encourage a new giving opportunity or event? The answer lies in getting prospects excited about your information throughout the year.

Here are a few suggestions for getting through the clutter:

- Make sure you are consistently sending valuable information to the same email address. And by *valuable*, I mean important to the recipient. If you are judiciously using email for weekly updates, activities, and exciting events (read: not too often to annoy), readers will look for your emails. If you overuse or abuse the relationship, into the spam box you go.
- Consider sending a postcard or a letter to anyone who has not opened one of your emails in the past six months. People don't want to think that you are watching their online habits too closely (although many organizations—nonprofit and otherwise—are doing just that), but explain that there are often last-minute invitations or ticket offers that only come through email. And make sure there *are* invitations and ticket offers from time to time. In other words, get them to whitelist you.

- To encourage people to open your emails, offer something offline that must be redeemed online or through a recent email. Maybe it is an offer that your donation will be matched if you use the code in your email. Or a free promotional product if you use the link in your email. Be creative but, again, make it benefit the donor more than the organization.
- Consider sending newsletters via email as well as in print. A good newsletter will provide a combination of personal stories, information, donor appreciation, and an up-to-date calendar. This is not to advocate completely switching over to online newsletters. Print newsletters get read by more people in the family unit and often hang around the house, like a magazine, encouraging browsing.

How to Suggest a Gift Amount

Specific language about how to suggest a gift amount is a common topic when we counsel nonprofits around soliciting gifts. Unfortunately, we cannot give you exact language because it needs to be in your voice. However, you can take the following suggestions as starting points. Then practice with a colleague until it sounds comfortable coming out of your mouth. And make sure you do not have to read from a paper to ensure you are saying it correctly.

- "I hope you will join me in supporting our annual fund this year. Last year you gave $500, but we were hoping that this year you would consider a gift of $750. Seven hundred and fifty dollars will help provide babysitting at Shabbat services for those who want to worship without a screaming toddler. Do you remember those days? Will you join me in making a gift to the annual fund of $750 today?"
- "You know that I have always been a passionate supporter of the synagogue and I would really like you to join me and become a Chai giver at the $1,800 level. Chai givers make an enormous impact by sponsoring the *oneg* for any Shabbat service that does not have a bar or bat mitzvah. Could you consider a gift of $1,800 today?"
- "Now that you have experienced the benefits of the religious school and your daughter has become a bat mitzvah at your

amazing *simcha* last year, I hope you will join me in supporting the education of our five hundred students a year with a gift of $5,400. Fifty-four hundred dollars will help sustain the seven community service off-sites the seventh graders were able to experience last year. Can you make that gift today?"

- "I know that your children are no longer in the religious school but that you still value Jewish education for each member of our community. Unfortunately, 10 percent of our students come from families who need assistance to pay the religious school fees. Would you consider a gift of $3,600 to provide a scholarship for one student this year?"

- "We have talked about all the exciting new programs like _____ that make our congregation so special. These programs only continue with the support of donors like you and me. Will you join me in making an annual fund gift of $3,600?"

Defining a Meaningful Gift

Anyone who has sat in a room rating prospects knows that it is hard to determine the right number for the ask. We can guess what a person is worth, determine what he has given to other organizations, examine his relationship with the synagogue, and estimate what he will give, but it is always questionable whether a person will give *that* much to *this* congregation.

If the intent to give a substantial gift is there, it is worth educating the prospect on what it means to give a meaningful gift.

The Background

For each person, the amount of a meaningful gift is different. Consider your own circumstances for a moment. Let us assume that there is a nonprofit organization with which you are involved besides the congregation. For the purpose of this exercise we'll call it Bounce. You have given to Bounce on an annual basis for the past five years. You believe in its mission and have gone to an event here or there because friends were going. Because the members of Bounce's development committee are good fundraisers, you are on their radar and since you understand the process, you know that you are being stewarded for a larger gift.

They set up a coffee for you and the executive director to get to know each other a little bit better and talk about your gift for the year. At the meeting, he asks you to make a meaningful gift by donating $XX,XXX. They consider that a meaningful gift, but all you can imagine is what your wife would say, since she is not involved with Bounce at all.

Meaningful Gifts: The Donor's Perspective

A meaningful gift is not necessarily the amount that Bounce has asked for, nor is it automatically twice or even three times that number. A meaningful gift is one that you would only give to a few chosen, special organizations. It should be within your budget, but it is a meaningful gift to you if it requires you to stop and think if that is the right amount, if you know this gift will genuinely help, if it will be crucial for the organization to reach its goals. A meaningful gift will give you the knowledge that you truly did all that you could do financially to help an organization.

Twenty-five thousand dollars may not be meaningful to some and $1,000 may be meaningful to others. But encouraging donors to think about what will have an impact—for the congregation and for themselves—will help strengthen the relationship between the donor and the synagogue, as well as encourage the donor to consider future giving.

Making a Presentation

Whether you are meeting with one donor or hosting a house party for twenty, presentation skills are essential.

Enthusiasm

Sometimes nerves get the best of us. The problem is not that someone might see that you are nervous. Rather, it is that what you are saying will get lost. The enthusiasm that can accompany your invitation to a prospect to join you in your campaign is contagious, as is fear of failure, desperation, or nervousness.

Practice on your coworkers, practice in front of your mirror, practice in your head. Record your presentation and listen to it. Do enough prep work to eliminate anything that will inhibit you from having confidence or exuding excitement when engaging an audience (written, in person, or over the phone).

A Smile

Presentations are best performed standing up with a smile on your face. The energy will be palpable. And your message has a better chance of being heard when people are actually listening instead of checking email or dozing due to a droning speaker. Something as simple as a smile and remaining vertical will remind you that you are in charge of the way you present.

Optimistic Attitude

You might question whether an optimistic attitude is the same as enthusiasm, but it can be the difference between cheering and coaching a game. Cheering requires enthusiasm and, oftentimes, a hope for success that everyone in the crowd and all the cheerleaders try to offer the players. But a coach must offer a pervasive sense of optimism that the team can win, that they have trained hard and have the ability to win, that they will succeed. If the coach doesn't believe it, neither will the players.

To bring the metaphor back to development, if you believe you can achieve your financial goals during your campaign, you stand a good chance at success. Don't sit on the sidelines and hope others will achieve your goals, because without your cheering and coaching (whether you are a volunteer or staff), they won't.

Being in the Moment

The idea of being in the moment is not a new concept, but it is more and more essential as distractions increase. Whether you are thinking about how your presentation is being perceived (it will be worse if that is what you are thinking about) or what's for dinner (drifting to other problems will not help you achieve your current goals), keeping yourself focused, present, and attentive will convey a positive impression. But getting distracted will definitely leave a negative feeling and reduce your chances of success.

There are, to be sure, many other ways to improve your presentation skills. For more ideas, pick up a top-rated sales book. You may not be selling widgets, but you are selling an idea of a strong Jewish community. And an idea is only as good as the people who are advocating on its behalf, who are selling the dream.

Scripting Your Meetings

The easiest way to decrease the anxiety surrounding an individual ask is to have a script. Preparing a script will require you to have an individual solicitation strategy and an amount you want to ask for. Having a script at a meeting will allow you to guide the flow of the conversation to reach the obvious conclusion.

Where do you start? Begin by clarifying your objectives. Pretend that you are a reporter and that you have to be sure that the lead—the first sentence of your story—answers the classic journalist's questions: who, what, when, where, why, and how. Once you know the facts consider:

- *Who* are you meeting with? Do you really know her and her relationship to the congregation as well as her giving history?
- *What* are you there to accomplish? Is this meeting the first in a series of planned events to cultivate and deepen the relationship? Or do you intend to solicit a gift?
- *When* will it feel right to move the conversation to the topic at hand—the gift or the request for greater involvement, such as joining the board?
- *Where* are you meeting? Is it a place where the prospective donor feels comfortable and in control of the environment?
- *Why* are you asking for a gift now? Has the prospect demonstrated that he is ready to make a commitment?
- *How* do you plan to open the conversation, turn it at the right moment, and ask for the gift?

Starting the Conversation

What will you do to get the prospect talking about herself? Do you share mutual interests or have friends in common? Were you both at an event recently that was especially good or remarkably bad? Write down details so that topic is front and center from the start. You want to create an easy conversation for the prospect from the moment you walk in the room.

Turning the Discussion Toward the Annual Fund

Does this prospect respond to general requests or is he more interested in the musical aspects of the congregation, for example? If it is music, what aspects are supported by the annual fund and could potentially be expanded with more stable funding? Be clear that you hope this is a gift for this year, not a onetime gift. Your synagogue depends on continued support.

The Ask

Know how much you will ask for and how you will phrase the ask (see some examples in "How to Suggest a Gift Amount" on page 122). Practice again and again until you feel comfortable with the phrasing.

Know what you will say if the prospect says no. What will you say to discover whether she is telling you *not yet* or *not ever*? How will you manage her concerns, especially if she articulates them in a very passionate way? Prepare yourself for different answers, acting them out with fellow solicitors.

Know what you will say if she says yes. Are there next steps that you can explain? For example, "After I hand in the pledge form, Robert in the office will send you a form to fill out to ask how you would like to be listed on the website and when you would like to be billed. Your receipt for tax purposes will not be sent until the January following the year in which the gift has been paid."

The End of the Meeting

How will you end your encounter? What expectations will the prospect or donor be left with? When do you expect to see him again? Remember to give him any promised follow-up. And absolutely send a personal note thanking the prospect (now hopefully a donor) for the time he took to meet with you.

By knowing what you want to say and anticipating how you will react to prospects' responses, you become unconsciously competent and prepared to listen actively to the person on the other side of the conversation. And once you can listen, you have a much better chance at success.

The Lost Art of Listening

Listening is an art and a skill. And in a world filled with self-promotion, it is becoming an ever-rarer skill. Here is your wake-up call to remember why, in fundraising, it is more important to listen than to talk.

People talk more than they listen. This problem is pervasive in modern society. Many of us don't listen because we're too busy talking, texting, blogging, and using Twitter and Facebook to give our point of view. We spend more time curating our images than paying attention to what the person next to us is talking about.

Because most people have become used to talking without listening, this tendency to transmit rather than receive has become the hallmark of the twenty-first century. The attitude that often characterizes our narcissistic society is "No view is as enlightened and informed as my view." We don't even bother to consider what others have to say.

That the ability to listen has lagged so much in this digital age, when the channels of communication have multiplied, seems ironic and counterproductive. And, in major-gifts fundraising—when you are face-to-face with your prospective donor—the failure to listen is a recipe for disaster.

When we are in a solicitation or cultivation meeting, a huge mistake too many of us make is to be so eager to make our point that we stop listening as we search for a way to dominate the conversation. Try to make a connection with the other person by sharing your experiences or showing you understand her point of view by recounting a story about someone in a similar situation.

When we listen, we communicate. How we listen determines how well we communicate, and how effectively we solicit or steward a donor.

Many of the most successful people in the world—whether in business, politics, the arts, or social relations—are good listeners. It is a skill that is rarely instinctive, but it can be learned. Here's how:

- Pay attention and do not be distracted. Serious conversation is never easy. Stay in the moment and listen attentively.
- Listen with intent. You must want to hear what the other person is telling you. You must be empathetic and focused on the other person.

- Do not be judgmental. A major duty of the listener/solicitor is to be open-minded and to reserve judgment.
- Exercise restraint. Be patient and do not interrupt. Be the relaxed, attentive listener who patiently waits, or is even gently encouraging. Then you may be the one who truly hears, overcomes the objection, and comes away with the gift.
- Express what you think or feel, but avoid being argumentative or aggressively competitive. Do not engage in intellectual one-upmanship.
- Never hesitate to ask for clarification or to restate what you've heard in your own words to make certain you heard what was intended. Done properly, this will tell the prospect you are truly listening and want to understand the points he's making.
- Be alert to coded messages. Sometimes, what you are being told is communicated less in words than in sighs, pauses, laughs, asides, gestures, tears, or facial expressions. Be aware of the total range of human communication.
- Observe body language and be mindful of your own. Leaning slightly forward implies both attention and interest, as does the occasional nod. Sitting or standing with your arms across your chest gives the impression that you are not interested or are being critical. Frowning or smiling inappropriately may send the signal that you are not really listening.

Listening is the single most powerful tool in your kit of fundraising skills, if you are willing to develop the skill.

If You Don't Ask, Someone Else Will

Let's be clear: Each member of your congregation is being asked to support other nonprofits. And the large majority—probably more than 90 percent—*are* actually supporting other nonprofits. So why don't they proactively give to your synagogue?

When polled, most members feel as if they already support the synagogue through dues and religious school fees. Dues are perceived as a required fee that was created to pay for the annual expenses of a congregation. The membership dues usually come with some benefits, but you can still go to services if you are not a member. You can still attend most classes if you are not a member. And you can still interact with a rabbi if you are not a member. In addition, donors feel that they are still giving *tzedakah* to the Jewish community even if they are not directly giving to the temple over and above their dues and fees.

So why should someone support the congregation above and beyond membership dues? If you can't offer a list of reasons, you shouldn't be asking her for support. Come up with the reasons the donor would want to support your congregation and ask her. Reluctance to meet face-to-face and ask her directly will make it easier for her to say yes when someone else asks her to increase her gift to another nonprofit organization.

Just because you don't ask for annual appeal support doesn't mean others have the same fear of asking. Prospects will be asked for small gifts from national nonprofits that purchased their names. They will be asked by friends to support causes to which they have little connection. And, if they have the capacity, they will be asked to give major gifts to other organizations on a regular basis.

Assuming they have chosen a finite amount to give to philanthropic organizations this year, they will reach that limit—with or without supporting your congregation. You can invite them to give or you can let fear of failure win out. But we can guarantee there is only one of those options that will help you reach increased levels of funding this year.

Overcoming Initial Objections

In fundraising you can often expect as many as six or seven no's before you get to yes. That number seems a bit shocking, and it might not always be a straightforward no you hear. It is your job to assess what the prospect is really saying. You can expect resistance if you are trying to change someone's perspective or hesitancy if you are asking him to dramatically change how he has done things in the past. The key is to understand what rejection means in nonprofit fundraising and consider how to overcome it.

Hearing *No*

This is not to suggest that you ask someone for a gift of $1,000 for the annual campaign, and that when she says no, you ask for the same amount six more times in exactly the same way. That will not be successful.

But you will rarely hear the word *no*. You will hear objections and concerns, and your job as a solicitor is to constantly work to overcome the initial objections—spoken or unspoken—to help the person get to yes.

Is the source of the prospect's objection:

- The dollar amount?
- The cause?
- The specific use of the funds (that is, he doesn't believe in the project)?
- That he has already given through dues?
- That he needs more information? (Some people respond to stories; others to data.)
- That he needs more time to consider?
- That a spouse or another family member or business partner needs to be a part of the process?
- That you should be asking the "other person"?
- That he is feeling less financially liquid because of a change in job, a fixed income, that retirement is either here or in sight, etc.
- That it is the wrong time for him personally?
- You? Are you the wrong solicitor?

Your goal is to overcome these objections—and perhaps others. What you are really hearing in these initial reactions is often *not now*, as opposed to *no, not ever*. Maybe she needs more cultivation or stewardship, more time or more understanding of the purpose of the appeal before she offers support.

Just don't give up when you hear the initial objection. Don't take it as a no. Listen carefully and consider how you can help him see that his objection is not insurmountable but just a reason to continue the conversation or to speak again in the near future. And then, most essentially, follow up.

There are four key steps to managing objections:

1. Clarify what the prospect is saying and be sure that you understand exactly what she means.
2. Acknowledge that you heard what the prospect is saying by repeating what she said, even using her exact same words.

3. Resume making the case for the gift, now focused like a laser only on the objection that the prospect has raised.

4. Close again, this time restating the gift in a different form—as an annual, quarterly, or a monthly amount.

While using these four tactics for managing objections, do not become argumentative. After acknowledging and responding to each objection, close again. Restate your request for the gift and wait quietly for a response, ready for the next objection or a commitment.

What kind of objections might you hear in a synagogue setting, and how might you respond?

- I like the rabbi, but I'm not sure I like what she talks about in her sermons. And she's not as inspirational as my childhood rabbi. I'm not sure I want to give money toward this rabbi.

  It is disappointing when the sermon does not speak to you, but there are so many aspects of the service besides the sermon, just as there are so many aspects of a synagogue beyond the service. If you don't find inspiration there, perhaps you would consider going to the Torah study, which I always find probes more deeply than a rabbi can do in one sermon.

- The temple looks good, but I hate the way you walk in. It feels so unwelcoming. Can I put money toward changing that instead of the annual fund?

  The entranceway has always been a bit of problem, but we hope you feel welcome inside the walls and among our community. We may, at some point, conduct a capital campaign if enough of us feel changes are required, but right now we are hoping you will join us in supporting the annual fund, which makes all those amazing programs possible as well as the kiddush lunch, which I know you would love. We all sit together and we make a special effort to welcome newcomers each week. Talk about welcoming! Can we count on your gift of $X,XXX for this year?

- I just don't have the money you are looking for right now. Maybe next year I can give something in that range.

While we would love it if everyone could afford to give $3,600 to the annual fund, we appreciate each and every gift. Do you think a gift of $1,800 would be possible? If you were to give monthly, that would work out to $150 a month.

As the solicitor, you should always seek to end the meeting with an agreement. If you do not achieve a commitment to give on the part of the prospect, at least agree to continue the conversation and set a time and place for your next meeting.

On the other hand, if a final gift decision has been made by the prospect, then restate the gift so the donor can hear you confirm the amount. Say *thank you* and congratulate the donor. Everyone should feel great about the shared accomplishment.

Overcoming the Stall

After months of cultivation and relationship building, the time has finally come to ask for that major gift of which all your research has told you that he is capable. At long last, you are face-to-face, knee-to-knee with the prospect. You know your prospect, your case, and that you are the right person to do the ask.

The setting is ideal. You have structured the environment so that the prospect really is comfortable and believes that he is in control. The conversation goes perfectly. You open and in a gentle way engage the prospect in the search for common ground. By responding to your open-ended questions, your prospect talks about himself and the congregation. As you listen actively and take notes, you are planning how to present the case for this prospect.

During the conversation, the prospect provides you with the perfect opening and you launch easily into the case. Even as you present your vision, you check in regularly with the prospect to make sure that he is with you every step of the way. Each time you ask an open-ended question, your prospect seems to become even more interested and invested in what you are saying. You are collecting a series of affirmative replies all along the way.

The moment of truth approaches, when you have to ask the prospect to do what you both came together to do, to make a difference. You ask the prospect to consider a gift of the rated amount. And after you ask, you are silent. The prospect turns the request over and over in his mind. You wait for the inevitable objections or excuses.

You are prepared for all sorts of objections. You have role-played with your colleagues every conceivable question that you think the prospect might raise.

And, so as not to disappoint you, the prospect does indeed ask some questions about the impact of his prospective gift, who else is contributing at this level, and what future needs would be.

You know how to respond. First, you seek clarification, if necessary, to make sure you understand exactly what the prospect is saying. Second, you acknowledge that you have heard what the prospect has said by restating the question. Then you resume the case in a focused manner to respond to the inquiry. And, finally, you close again by asking the prospect to consider the gift, stated perhaps in a different manner than initially.

Finally, after what has seemed like an eternity, but in reality is only a few seconds, the prospect says, "I'd like to think it over." You have just encountered the "stall." The good news is that the prospect does have some desire to make the gift; after all, he came this far in the solicitation process with you. The bad news is that something is stopping him from making a gift decision now.

A stall signals conflict. The conflict is the agony of indecision between the desire to make the gift and feelings of uncertainty and anxiety. When the desire is great enough, the prospect will make the gift. A stall usually means your prospect does not have enough reason to buy now; he does not have a sense of the opportunity or the urgency. You obviously need to do something.

You remember all the affirmative responses you "collected" during the earlier part of the conversation. Now, in the face of the stall, you need to focus on the prospect's positive emotions about your congregation and the gift opportunity. When you overcame the objections earlier in the conversation, you neutralized a block in the decision-making process. However, that is not enough. To overcome the stall, the prospect must feel a strong positive benefit. Your task is to discover what the prospect perceives those benefits are and help him focus on them. Tell him you understand and then help him work through his indecision by asking questions such as:

- What do you find exciting about this synagogue?
- What advantage do you see in the opportunity?
- How would you benefit from making the gift?

By eliciting answers to such questions, you will gain a clearer understanding of your prospect's motivation and be in a better position to move him toward a positive decision.

Try to find out the reason the prospect feels he might need more time to "think about it." Then when the prospect identifies his reasons for not making a positive decision, you have an opportunity to deal with them.

The best way to overcome stalls is to focus the prospect on his positive thoughts and identify the blocks. You may find that the prospect wants to give but does not see why he should do so now. He may not feel the urgency.

It is up to you to create that sense of urgency by "selling" his problem back to him. Build his desire by reminding him of the problem, the benefits to him and the congregation that his gift will provide, and all the possible consequences of inaction. Get agreement on the opportunity, then rescue him with the solution—all the positive benefits that he had identified earlier.

Of course, there are times when you are legitimately stalled. For example, you and the prospect must do further analysis of the cash flow needs of the project as well as the income and estate tax consequences of the gift. In that case, you must employ strategies to obtain the next appointment as you keep his interest and involvement high.

Whether on the first or the final call, the stall is the classic excuse to avoid making the gift decision. With a bit of practice, you can become adept at questioning to uncover the reason for the stall. In that way, you will help the prospect understand why he can benefit from making the gift commitment today.

PART V

How Great Fundraising Will Improve Your Synagogue Culture

Chapter 14

Stewardship
The Path to Donor Retention

What Is Stewardship?

According to the *Merriam-Webster Dictionary*, *stewardship* is defined as:

1. The office, duties, and obligations of a steward
2. The conducting, supervising, or managing of something; *especially* the careful and responsible management of something entrusted to one's care

Do you get a giddy feeling when you see an envelope in the office that you know contains a donation? By opening that envelope (or waiting for the staff person to do the honors), you are becoming the person in charge of conducting, supervising or managing, and stewarding the gift. You are taking on the care and responsibility of the financial contribution, as well as the relationship with the donor. This is stewardship.

In fundraising, stewardship is the postgift equivalent of cultivation before the gift. It is the series of events that takes place after the gift in order to ensure a satisfied donor as well as a repeat donor. And while it may feel like a lot of work to steward your donors, as we said before, it is 4½ times harder and more expensive to acquire a new donor than to retain an existing donor.

Why You Should Steward Your Donors

Consider your fifty largest donors. What would you do if they stopped giving? Without stewardship, you are relying on the donors to keep up the connection. You are assuming that a couple of letters a year, maybe a phone call, will be enough to keep those checks coming. But each year that you do the bare minimum to engage these donors, you are taking the chance that another organization will treat them well and they will shift their philanthropic priorities away from your congregation.

On the other hand, if you are asking a donor for a long-term investment in your congregation, you should be prepared to invest time and energy in that donor.

Easy Money

We live in a society that encourages immediate and instant gratification. Everyone has an amount—easy money—they give when they feel they have to donate something to a cause that they aren't really committed to. Your sister-in-law is running the marathon and needs to raise $5,000 for nonprofit X. Your friend's parent dies and donations in his memory are requested for organization Y. Your colleague invites you to a fundraising event for a nonprofit and you just can't say no. For some people it is $25; for others it is $100; and for still others, it may even be as much as a $1,000. But it is almost always a onetime gift. You are not looking for onetime gifts or easy money.

You want the donor to feel excited about the interaction that she had with you surrounding this gift and thrilled with the opportunity to have made a philanthropic investment in the future of the congregation. But beyond that, you want to find ways to engage the donor even more deeply. That deeper connection can be found through moves management and stewardship (more on moves management can be found in the next chapter). You want all your donors to feel more connected and involved in the congregation, knowing they are helping the synagogue reach new heights—even if they rarely come to services.

One Year at a Time

Make stewardship the priority for one fiscal year. What if you retain 5 percent more donors than you did the previous year? Then contributions by new donors, who usually make up for any lost donors, would really constitute new donations. It would improve your numbers, and build confidence that you are pushing the needle in the right direction.

Stewardship has other benefits besides securing and retaining financial support. Looking for new board members? You can use your knowledge of synagogue donors to figure out who might be ready to increase their involvement. Smaller volunteer opportunities, from honorees at annual events to committee members, are easier to find when there is a large pool of people who feel they are involved with and respected by the organization.

The essence of an annual fund major gifts program is not a set of financial goals alone. That is shortsighted. The ultimate goal is to build a group of individual lifelong donors who feel strongly committed to your congregation. Lifelong donors who are lifelong members. Lifelong members who don't see the dues or donations as the burden of being Jewish, but as something that makes them feel even better about their commitment to Judaism.

How You Should Steward Your Donors

Stewardship requires you to continually connect with the donor. How you "touch" each donor depends on your synagogue's culture, the donor's capacity, and your ultimate goals. Here is an overview of some of the methods to consider.

Communications

You are not communicating with a donor if your only points of contact are appeal letters. That is a solicitation. Communication means that you are informing her of something you think is interesting or want to communicate with her. You're not just providing a few facts at the same time that you are asking for an additional gift.

You should publish a newsletter. In it, you can offer general progress reports by mentioning the more exciting aspects of the annual fund. If the annual fund contributes to kiddush lunches or helps five of the twenty-five new member families abate dues, mention that in an article. (For example, "Thank you to the annual fund for supporting the kiddush lunches when there are no b'nai mitzvah," or "Thanks to the annual fund, we were able to encourage five families to join our congregation this quarter, regardless of their ability to pay full dues.") Then you can call a major donor and ask if he saw the article and how glad you were that his gift helped encourage new membership.

Do you send out updates through email? Why not offer a brief email with an image of LED bulbs in February. "This year we were able to abate dues for thirty-five families and twenty-seven seniors. To show our appreciation to those who supported the annual fund and helped these families feel comfortable in our community—regardless of their income level—we have also replaced sixty-two (35 + 27) light-bulbs with LEDs throughout the building. Thanks to the annual fund we have a stronger community that has reduced our carbon footprint and made less of an environmental impact. To see a list of those who have helped this vision become reality CLICK HERE. To find out more about how gifts like yours to the annual fund impact our synagogue, email Jessica@thebesttemple.org."

Have an interesting event that was supported by the annual fund? Send a personal note to your annual fund donors reminding them that their gift helped create this opportunity for the community. Maybe you want to call your top fifty donors and personally invite them to the event and thank them again for their support.

How do these ideas steward donors? It shows them how their money is being spent and that you are aware that it is your responsibility to manage their gifts wisely. It thanks them an additional time for their support. And it helps them feel good about the gift they have already given, which makes them more likely to give a gift in the future.

Engagement

Donors who also volunteer their time are more invested in the relationship. Not everyone can serve on the board, but there are many other ways to get involved in a synagogue as a volunteer. Would they want to provide meals (store-bought or homemade) to those who are sitting shiva? Would they like to host the scholar-in-residence dinner? Would they be interested in handing out Chanukah candles to the religious school students?

Every time you encourage someone to be involved beyond her checkbook, you are encouraging a deeper connection to the synagogue, which makes her more likely to continue to donate. Such engagement will benefit the community at the same time it improves the bottom line.

Conversation

One of the large advantages of major donor status is that organizations ask you for your opinion, instead of waiting for you to offer your ideas.

Start with your top twenty-five donors and consider how and when to call and ask for their opinion. You can make the questions general: "Have you had any recent experiences that you have particularly enjoyed or disliked and would be interested in sharing with the leadership?" Or specific questions: "We noticed you attended our movie night last month. We are considering what we can do to increase attendance. Do you have any suggestions that would make the night more appealing or more enjoyable?" This opens dialogue for a conversation, eliciting a response.

Be prepared for negative answers. These might not feel good to hear, but it is important for the leadership to hear them. This is true even if the person has voiced such an opinion before. If you stick your head in the sand, the donor will still be dissatisfied and potentially decrease giving. Or, worse, leave the congregation. So how do you handle a strong negative response? Do not get confrontational. You can work together to brainstorm solutions, you can offer to have the rabbi or president have the conversation, or you can say that you understand that he has been feeling this way for some time. Unfortunately, not everyone agrees, so maybe it is time to focus on more positive aspects of his relationship with the synagogue.

Twenty-five donors sounds like a lot at first. But this is not a short-term project. Could the development staff fit in two calls a week? Even if you eliminate the weeks surrounding the High Holidays and vacation time, that would still enable you to increase contact to ninety donors a year. Ninety donors who will feel better about their gift and continue to donate—potentially at a higher level.

Some donors will tell you that they are not interested in talking on the phone or meeting at the office, and that's okay too. Stewardship is about reaching the donor where she is, not about where you want her to be.

Building Routine into Stewardship

Adding the two calls a week makes things manageable. Consider how to build routine into all aspects of your stewardship.

- Have board members make thank-you calls once a year. Schedule it so that it happens every January. (Most people have never received a call from a nonprofit to simply thank them for their support. One evening and some board members, each with their cell phone, are all that is required to make donors feel good about how their gifts have affected your organization.)

- Send donors articles about the synagogue—whether written by you or by the press—three times a year.
- Encourage donors to attend events that have been supported by the annual fund at least two times this year.
- Find three board members who will each set up coffee with one major donor every month to offer an update.

The top ninety donors would then receive at least one call, three emails or snail mail letters, two event invitations, and one coffee. That is six times donors are reminded that you are grateful for their gift and would like to retain the relationship.

Even if they do not attend an event or follow through with the coffee, they will know they are valued and you will be stewarding them toward a stronger relationship with the synagogue.

Who Should Steward Your Donors?

You. The rabbi(s). The executive director. Board members. Development staff. Every leader in the congregation should be involved in stewardship. Unless you have a large development staff (and few congregations do), this responsibility is too overwhelming for one staff member or a few board members. It requires the commitment of many people. One person can write an interesting update and another can write a personal note on the front of that update. One person can create a nonfundraising event and someone else can make a call to invite donors. One person can write a script for a thank-you call and another can host the thank-a-thon. There are so many ways to support stewardship that being shy or being afraid to ask is never an excuse for not getting involved.

Have You Ever Been Stewarded?

Do you donate to any nonprofits on a consistent basis? If so, you have probably been stewarded. And if you are aware of how you are stewarded, you can consider what aspects of that process helped you feel good about your gift. Then you might incorporate those into your new stewardship policies.

Consider the last few gifts you have given to any nonprofit for any reason. Take a minute and think about the interactions you have with those organizations since the gift.

- How quickly did you receive a thank-you note?
- Was anything included with the note (such as information about the organization or information about how the gift was used)?
- Was there something that made you feel especially connected to the organization that would help encourage an additional gift? What was it?
- Were you considered a major donor for any of the gifts?
- Were you treated differently than you were after giving smaller gifts?
- Did you like how you were treated?
- Was there anything you thought should or could have been done to engage you further or deepen your relationship?
- Did you stop giving to one or more of these organizations? If so, why?

A strong organization does not let anyone slip through the cracks. At least, the organization tries to keep its donors involved.

If you cannot remember how a gift was handled, conduct a test. Go to a gala or a house party. Sign up to volunteer at a walk. Give to the next walk/run/bike-a-thon, and see what happens next. Do you think the response you got was an appropriate way to encourage a future gift or did it feel like too much or too little? You will then know what you like—which is not to say that you will know what others like. But it will help you determine what steps to take next.

Events as Opportunities for Donor Acquisition

Stewarding those who have attended a special event as their first contact with your congregation does not mean importing their names into your membership list and hoping they will join and that they will give when they receive the appeal letter.

People go to lectures or galas for a variety of reasons, but a large number of newbies are friends of the honorees. And the majority of those friends don't know or care about your synagogue. But you have one night and various means of follow-up that can pique their interest and retain these prospective members and donors.

Create special pieces based on something that happened at the event or something they purchased at the silent auction. In one piece, highlight the honoree as a continuing supporter and ask these prospects to join in making a real impact. Invite them to other events that attract a similar demographic or a large event that might just appeal to them.

They may never give again, but at least they will know why their friend is involved in such an amazing congregation.

Chapter 15

Moves Management

A Disciplined Approach to Securing Major Gifts

Moves management is a process in which you take a series of steps (moves) in an attempt to move each individual prospect to action—to move to the next gift.

Defining a Move

Each move represents a contact, by whatever means:

- Email
- Phone call
- Letter
- Fax
- Face-to-face conversation
- Planned events

Moves involve cultivation, not solicitation. To be successful, you should plan one move a month, or twelve a year.

The Goal of Each Move

When you're cultivating a prospect, it is hard to "quantify" goals. In moves management, you should consider what you are hoping to achieve. Be specific but realistic—you will not attain a major gift in three moves if you are starting from zero. However, you can hope to determine whether this is a true major gift prospect after three moves.

Here are some sample goals of a move:

- Your prospect accepts an invitation to a program visit.
- You gain a better sense of how the prospect feels about the synagogue.
- You determine if the pace of the moves and the goal are correct for this particular prospect.

Planning Each Move

There are a number of steps to take when you plan each move:

1. Review key points to cover during the move.
2. List benefits that will appeal to the prospect.
3. Specify the action you are asking the prospect to take—that is, the next step in the process.
4. List questions you anticipate the prospect will ask, as well as your answers.

Then determine who participates in the process.

- The *leader* is the prospect's relationship or moves manager, generally a member of the development staff.
- Next is the *primary player*, a person the prospect is not able to say no to. This might be a friend, a colleague, or a perceived peer.
- Then you need to identify *natural partners*—people who can serve as sources of information, with strong relationships with the prospect. These may be people who offered insight during prospect research or who have surfaced as close friends. They may also ensure that your data is up-to-date.
- Finally, you should seek *centers of influence*, who have information to share about the prospect but may not have access to or a relationship with her.

Each member of this micro-development team is there because of who the individual prospect is. And each team is likely to be different, depending on the prospect.

Role of the Relationship or Moves Manager

The moves manager—an experienced major gifts officer who is a staff member of your synagogue—may have the responsibility for one hundred or more prospects at any one time, each of whom is at a different stage of development. The moves manager creates a strategy for each prospect, tracks the prospect's relationship to the congregation, plans moves, and coordinates the primary players and the natural partners, as well as any centers of influence. Above all, the moves manager is responsible for executing the individual prospect's plan. If circumstances warrant, the moves manager reconfigures the strategy and continually refines the plan.

Instead of considering this approach overwhelming, you should see moves management as a process that enables you to manage your time and the resources of your team. It focuses the long-term goals into short-term steps to turn a donor into a major donor or a major donor into a sustaining donor who has made a planned gift or a multiyear commitment. It may require additional staff, but it will result in significantly better outcomes.

Creating a Moves Management Strategy

You might find that this section is similar to other disciplined processes mentioned throughout this book. That is no coincidence. We are offering a new way for you to think about every aspect of successful fundraising. In this section, the focus is on individual major gift prospects. Once you have donors, they should be shifted into stewardship and moves management.

This six-step implementation strategy and methodology will guide you through the process. The first three steps help you enlist major donor prospects who will be the focus of your moves management. Start with the identification of prospects, then gather information through prospect research—formal and informal—and, finally, evaluate each prospect to determine that he is worth allocating the time and energy of staff and volunteer leadership. The last three steps focus on the application of your findings through tracking moves, maintaining accountability, and reporting your findings.

Step 1: Identify Prospects

Begin by reviewing your current database of donors. Screen for frequency of giving, how recently they donated, those who increase their gifts annually, and possibly the "diamonds in the rough"— high-net-worth individuals who have demonstrated interest in an area in which your congregation excels, such as inclusion of those who learn differently. This would be a good time to conduct an electronic prospect research screening of your identified prospects to determine wealth as well as philanthropic and political giving patterns—sure markers of value for further consideration. Then engage your board collectively—and, better still, individually—to identify sources of information about and relationships with the prospects through the internal prospect screening process described in chapter 8.

Step 2: Gather Partners

Whether or not a board member or a community leader is active on the development committee, he can still be your best partner. Prospective partners are people who are invested in the success of your fundraising—even if they aren't interested in working on the process. These natural partners will deepen their relationship with the synagogue by being engaged in this way.

Set up an appointment and, when you meet, share a list of prospective donors—people whom you believe could be major donor prospects. Ask him:

- What is the prospect's gift capacity rating?
- Do you have access to this prospect? Will she return your call?
- Can you share information about this prospect?

This extends the internal prospect screening beyond the scope of the development committee and into a broader community of leaders of the congregation.

Step 3: Evaluate Prospects

Once you have met with your board members—and your colleagues on the staff—collate all the information that you have gathered. This is where you pool together all your data to make the determination as to whether or not this person is a legitimate major donor prospect and what you plan to do to move this prospect toward a major gift.

You are seeking to answer questions like these:

- Why is this individual a prospect?
- In what areas has this person expressed interest?

- For what purposes should funding be sought?
- What is her giving capacity?
- What is our present relationship? (Review her prior gifts and involvement.)
- Who are partners/centers of influence?

You and your team should go through your list and agree on the prospects with whom you wish to move forward strategically and tactically.

> *Note: There will be some prospects you wish were on this list but are lacking the connection or incentive at this time. Keep those names on a second list or code them differently in your software. Consider what needs to change before you can add them to your major-prospects list. Is it a deeper connection with the rabbi? Is it something that is out of your control (for example, they dislike the music that was added to services—even though the rest of the congregation loves the new sound)? Is it their lack of connection with other members? If you truly want them to be donors, it may take work that is outside the development committee's purview. Who will be charged with bringing this group into the fold?*

Now it is time to develop a detailed plan of background and foreground moves for each prospect. Background moves are designed for people because they are part of a group—for example, those who have given $500 or more at any one time in the last two years, or all the parents of children in the religious school who have the capacity to make a gift of $5,000 or more. Foreground moves are steps designed with a specific individual in mind, such as a visit with the rabbi to discuss a new initiative in social justice in an area of interest to that one person.

Step 4: Track Moves—The Call Report

After the moves for the next three to six months are planned, the single most critical step in the process is tracking each move and the follow-up step that is essential to the plan's implementation. This step requires exquisite discipline. With each discrete move or contact, you need to file a call report, a sample of which can be found on page 173 in Appendix 2.

Here is the data you need to keep track of:

- Type of call
  - ❏ Letter
  - ❏ Phone
  - ❏ Email
  - ❏ Tweet or other social media contact
  - ❏ In person
- Planned purpose of the move
  - ❏ Cultivation
  - ❏ Solicitation
  - ❏ Other (specify)
- Summary, with detailed notes specifying the outcome of the move
- Next steps
  - ❏ Retain this donor on the moves management list
  - ❏ Remove from moves management list
  - ❏ Reassign to another moves manager

Step 5: Maintain Accountability—The Weekly Report

Weekly, biweekly, and/or monthly face-to-face meetings of the major-gifts management team, with reports by each moves manager, are essential for tracking progress and maintaining accountability. This may be the development staff and the development committee, the development staff and the executive team, or some combination of staff and volunteers who are charged with the success of the annual fund. The frequency of these meetings is a function of the availability of the members of the team and the number of prospects in the process.

> Note: The purpose of this check-in is to know if you are making progress. If fewer people begin to attend these meetings or they keep getting canceled, the group is saying moves management is not a fundraising priority.
>
> These moves are essential to moving donors into the major donor category to achieve your goal of greater financial sustainability for the congregation. A lack of regular meetings implies that you are hoping that you will improve your synagogue's fundraising without doing the work. And, hope is not a strategy.
>
> If you have come this far in learning how to improve the results of your annual appeal, this is where you have to decide how impor-

tant a stronger annual fund is to you. It will take work, regular meetings, and the drive to convince your community that you are making this a priority.

Before each meeting, a report should be distributed containing the following data (a sample of which can be found on page 174 in Appendix 2):

- Prospect name and unique identifier in your fundraising data management system
- Philanthropic capacity rating
- Pipeline status—where the prospect is on the moves management continuum (and the likelihood of closing the gift)—the five *I's*
  - You have just *identified* a potential major gifts donor (10 percent likelihood of closing the gift)
  - You are gathering *information* about the prospect (25 percent likelihood of closing the gift)
  - You have begun to move the prospect to increase his *interest* in the congregation (50 percent likelihood of closing the gift)
  - The prospect has responded and become *involved* (75 percent likelihood of closing the gift)
  - The prospect has made a gift and become *invested* (100 percent likelihood of closing the gift)
- Date of last contact
- Nature of contact
- Next step
- Comments from moves manager/team

Step 6: Keep Score—Major Gifts Management Dashboard

Finally, create a congregation-wide dashboard for the major gifts moves management process. In this way everyone becomes a partner and shares in the success of the effort. The dashboard should contain the following (see the sample form on page 175 in Appendix 2):

- Date of report
- Total number of prospects in the system
- Total number of moves planned for the year
- Number of moves made this week

- Dollar value of prospects moved this week
- Number and dollar value of pledges or gifts booked this week and year-to-date, as compared to the same week last year

Then you can have individual sheets for each of the moves managers with the list of the relationships they are managing. This can be done on an Excel spreadsheet or a Google Doc as easily as anything else, but make sure you know who has access to make changes and that one person is master of the list.

The Discipline of Execution

The best plans in the world require a discipline of execution that ensures successful implementation and the desired outcomes. Major gifts management, as we have detailed, is a series of steps (moves) for each identified prospect. The plan begins by gaining the prospect's attention and stimulating a deeper interest in your congregation. You are moving the donor toward the goal—that she develops a desire to take an action, that is, make a major gift. And then you retain her attention through thoughtful, well-planned individualized steps of stewardship to keep her continually moving toward the next gift.

Now it is time to turn to the most important aspect of any plan—implementation. Here is a methodology to execute the plan, based on the Franklin-Covey Four Disciplines of Execution.

1. Focus on Wildly Important Goals (WIGs)

To execute a plan, you need to be absolutely focused on the right objective. The first principle is to narrow the focus of your goals, ideally choosing one quantifiable goal, but definitely not more than two quantifiable goals.

Another consideration is to make sure that the focus is on what's important and urgent. Here are some examples of strategic goals from which you might choose:

- Number of gifts of $5,000+ increased by XX percent
- Number of new gifts at $5,000+
- Amount of money in gifts of $5,000+ as compared to last year
- Increase of all $1,000+ donors' gifts by XX percent

2. Act on Lead Measures

The second principle is to act on what is forward-looking, is within your control, and impacts the outcome. We call that a "lead measure," or an activity that enables you and your team to achieve your wildly important goal. You should differentiate between the lead measure, which indicates whether you are likely to achieve your goal, and a lag measure, which, as its name implies, describes what you have achieved through an action completed in the past.

3. Keep a Compelling Scoreboard

Keeping score—and letting everyone who is working to improve fundraising see it—is the third key principle of execution. The scoreboard is simple and graphically visual. It is dynamic and is updated on a regular basis. Use the scoreboard to keep track of lead measures, such as:

- Complete four quality visits per staff person per week
- Ask for something on each visit
- Document quality follow-up after each visit within forty-eight hours

4. Create a Cadence of Accountability

Finally, once you have established your goal and your lead measures, you should create and maintain a system of accountability through weekly meetings. In these recurring meetings, everyone reports on past performance during the prior week and announces plans for the coming week's activities. This is where plan execution actually happens. It is accomplished through shared accountability.

At least weekly, we *account* by reporting on prior commitments, *review* the scoreboard to learn from our successes and failures, and *plan* to clear the path and make new commitments.

We make commitments and are accountable to ourselves, each other, the team, our supervisor, and the congregation. In this way, through a carefully crafted plan that is well executed, we achieve the important goal we have set for the sustainability and growth of the synagogue.

Thirty Moves Management Ideas

It is not easy to start from scratch and create individualized plans that focus your energy on moving donors toward a major gift. There are many types of moves you and your team can make, but here are seven categories that will hopefully aid you in considering what goals you will achieve with each move.

While far from comprehensive, this list should enable you to find twelve moves (from the thirty listed below) for each of your prospects to include in your donor-centric plan for the next year (ideally at least one a month).

- Moves that establish meaningful contact:
    1. Name a donor as host for an event
    2. Email the donor some specific program notes that you think may appeal to him
    3. Make a personal call thanking the donor for a gift
    4. Recognize the donor at an event
    5. Publicly thank the donor for a previous gift at an event, in a congregational email or newsletter, or highlight her on the website
- Moves that provide new information for the donor (attaching a personal note strengthens the relationship and creates a chance for response):
    6. Newsletters
    7. Personalized email
    8. Clipping and then mailing a prospect an article related to a recent conversation
    9. Videos produced for or by program participants who are beneficiaries of the annual fund
- Moves that provide new information to the congregation about the donor:
    10. Coffee/lunch/drinks
    11. Volunteer forms
    12. Invitation to attend an event where all attendees will be asked to fill out basic information forms
    13. Phone calls to invite prospects to an upcoming event

- Moves that deepen the connection:
  14. Create a unique, interactive experience with the congregation's program beneficiaries
  15. Ask the prospect to host an event at his house
  16. Nominate the prospect to the board
  17. Invite him to be on the host committee
  18. Ask her to speak on behalf of the congregation at a community forum
  19. Offer him a behind-the-scenes tour of the preschool or space to be renovated for a new program underwritten by the annual fund
- Moves that help present the case for giving:
  20. Ask for her opinion on your "draft" case for giving (which will always remain a draft)
  21. Ask for his opinion on your strategic plan
  22. Participate in a confidential interview to determine interest in and capacity for giving
  23. Personally invite her to an event that highlights the case for giving
- Moves that help introduce donors to the synagogue leadership:
  24. Set up a meeting with the executive director/program staff/board chair/rabbi
  25. Invite him to private or special events
  26. Ask if she is interested in joining a specific committee
- Moves that lead to and may result in an ask and/or gift:
  27. Make a stewardship move for a previous gift (see chapter 14)
  28. Make a follow-up phone call after a recent event
  29. Personally express your appreciation for the donor's time and money
  30. Initiate a conversation with the donor inquiring about friends or colleagues he thinks could help support the organization

The specifics are up to you. Your congregation may have distinctive activities that can be used to move and steward donors, and you should use every one of them. You know that your synagogue is unique—even if the way to bolster fundraising is not.

Chapter 16

The Cycle Repeats

As we mentioned at the beginning of this book, fundraising is part of development. Development is the path to finding new prospects and retaining current donors; it is a cycle that must be continually refreshed to ensure financial security for your synagogue. We have talked about engaging your community in the process, the development plan, the role of volunteers and staff (including clergy), tools for donor engagement, the ask, stewardship, and moves management. But all of this assumes that your members are already donors. What if only 30 percent of the congregation donates to the annual fund? How do you help the rest of the congregation feel that they should give above and beyond the dues?

Stage 1: Gateway Events—Welcoming the Prospective Donor into the Fundraising Process

A gateway is not a single event or house party designed to find new donors. A gateway is a disciplined four-stage plan intended to engage individual prospects and donors for an enhanced annual fund. It is the consideration of the steps before, during, and after a short informational event. It is a way to deepen the relationship with current donors while bringing their friends and colleagues into the fold. It is the gateway for individuals to enter into your donor community.

The first stage of the plan is designed to introduce or reintroduce people to your synagogue. This is not a new member presentation about the weekly services or a get-to-know-the-rabbi event. Instead, it is an introduction to the programs, people, and the *je ne sais quoi* that makes your synagogue special. It may seem as if everyone has this information, but many people in any given congregation do not feel like they are "insiders."

We call these initial gatherings gateway events. For the prospective donor, a gateway event serves as the first point in a cycle of lifelong giving. Such an event, for current and lapsed donors, can also reintroduce the person to what is currently happening in the community—what aspects of inclusion you have incorporated into your religious school, or what unique programs you were able to offer this year.

Imagine a breakfast meeting onsite, a luncheon in a board member's conference room, or a wine-and-cheese reception in a donor's home. Ten to fifteen prospective donors have been identified by board or development committee members and have been invited to gather to learn more about the synagogue beyond the liturgical. There will be no solicitation of funds—all you are seeking to do is to introduce high-net-worth individuals to the important work that you do.

The invitation is issued by each prospect's primary player and that person attends as well. There are three basic components to the gateway:

- Capturing names and contact data with permission of the prospect.
- Presenting a well-prepared, succinct overview of the mission, vision, and values of the congregation; its work; the costs of doing that work; the outcomes of fulfilling the mission and achieving the vision; and finally the opportunities for people to engage with you.
- Including a compelling, emotional hook. After all, we are all emotional donors. While we seek rational reasons to justify our decision to give, that decision is essentially an emotional one.
- Doing follow-up to keep these prospects engaged.

Here are some examples of emotional hooks in the congregation setting:

- A fifteen-year-old explains that the synagogue's post–b'nai mitzvah classes and youth group activities are the places where she feels most at home. While the youth lounge is nothing special to look at, she has found community there—people around whom she can be herself. And while not all their events are overtly

Jewish, her Jewish identity keeps her involved. It is young Jews having fun with other Jews.

- A widowed fifty-something notes that she found support from the congregation at every step of the process—from guidance at shiva and meals during mourning to new friends and meetings at the synagogue that have been helping her heal and face the new realities of her situation.
- Through the hikes on Shabbat morning, a new member met twenty to thirty environmentally like-minded members. He also found camaraderie during the once-a-month walks through local parks.
- A member points out the impact that working at the homeless shelter with his fellow congregants has made on his life. Making that a regular part of his schedule—even once every other month—has kept him tethered to *tikkun olam* in a spiritual and concrete way. The opportunity to volunteer with the synagogue made it easy and accessible and he is proud to be a part of the community.
- The adult Hebrew class gave a member the confidence to read Torah on Yom Kippur this year—thirty-five years after her bat mitzvah. This experience was just as meaningful because it was something she chose. Two other members of her class chanted this year as well.

Stage 2: Consciously Cultivating These Prospective Lifelong Donors

If the gateway event plants seeds in the minds and hearts of prospects and donors, then during the second stage you consciously begin the process of cultivation through a series of follow-up moves that are designed to involve these people in synagogue life.

Building lifelong donors is a process that, once begun, never ends. You are constantly creating new prospects and donors to be stewarded. And whether you are cultivating the "never-evers" or those who are already in your pipeline, you cannot forget or ignore any of them. If you do, that will be seen as a sign that you are disorganized and unworthy of investment.

The key to the success of the gateway event is calling every prospect who was present within forty-eight hours after the event. These calls should be made by the person who invited each prospective donor to the event.

Every follow-up call is essentially a personal contact asking for feedback. You might even view such a contact as a systematic market research call. The questions for which you are seeking answers are these: "What will it take to have this prospective donor feel that he has made a real contribution?" and "To what extent does he want to become involved?"

When you engage a prospective donor through a follow-up call, it enables you to create a customized plan for each one. And the sooner you can connect and ask for feedback, the sooner you can give the prospective donor what she wants so that she keeps coming back for more—and ultimately makes the gift that begins or continues the process of becoming a lifelong donor.

Preparation and a script for such follow-up calls are helpful. They allay some of your concerns regarding what you will talk about or what is essential to achieving your goals.

Here is a sample script that you might use with a prospective donor to learn how he might want to become involved. And just as important as the script is your ability to listen actively for cues that the prospect will provide. (If you do not remember why listening is so essential, reread "The Lost Art of Listening" on page 128.)

After you have reached the person with whom you wish to speak, identified yourself, and asked permission to speak for a moment or two, you might begin by saying:

Thank you for coming to our gateway event. What did you think?

Then be quiet and listen.

Is there any way you could see yourself becoming more involved with our congregation?

Then be quiet and listen.

(Note: When you ask someone about becoming more involved with the congregation, you should be prepared with two or three options if he asks you what "involvement" might look like.)

Is there anyone else you think we should invite to another gateway event like the one you attended?

Then be quiet and listen.

If you have listened well, you will have learned how to plan a "campaign of one" to engage, interest, and involve this prospect in a way that leads to a philanthropic investment and the journey toward life-long support.

Can You Follow Up by Email?

Yes and no. If you are using email to ensure that everyone there gets a point of contact within twenty-four or forty-eight hours because Shabbat is coming and the calls might spread into seventy-two or ninety-six hours, then yes. If you are using it to avoid making phone calls, then no.

A general email sent to all attendees, even with their name in it, lacks the personalization of a call or a handwritten note. Mention a particular aspect of a conversation you had, answer a question that came up, or point out that you're sorry you didn't have time to have a one-on-one conversation and you hope to meet up again soon. That is the way to be remembered. And that is the way to move a donor toward a major gift.

Making the Call

Pick up the phone. Do not be afraid. Keep in mind that there are only a few possible outcomes:

- The person answers the phone and you have a lovely conversation.
- You get voice mail, leave a message, and mention that you will try back during the next day or two (which you must do or you'll lose credibility for yourself and the congregation).
- The person answers and says she does not want to speak to you about it. Then, as the person who extended the original invitation and accompanied the prospect to the event, you need to learn more about what happened. This is where the major gifts management team can be helpful. Bring the case there and brainstorm what might be done to engage with this person. And remember, it just may be that this is a case of *no, not now*. Then thank her and turn your time and energy to another prospect.

In this day and age, with caller ID and voice mail, the person who answers the phone is willing to have a conversation. Yay! If a prospect doesn't answer after a few attempts, put him onto a list to be contacted in the future through a different path of engagement. You want to find new donors who are excited about giving. You do not want to twist arms or guilt people into anything.

Stage 3: Making the Ask

When the prospective donor is ready, you move very naturally to the third stage; you make the ask. Are you ready? You will need to overcome your own fears and anxieties, which are completely natural. Fear of the unknown outcome, fear of undermining a friendship, fear of having to change tactics on the spot, fear of getting a gift far below what your team has deemed as the donor's capacity, fear of failure, and even fear of success can all get in the way of your progress. Once you overlay our general fear of asking for *anything* with our cultural neurosis about money, you can understand why people refuse to make a solicitation.

The irony is that even if you are afraid of fundraising, the donor is often ready to make a gift before the solicitor asks. Because, again, you are not the first person to ask this donor for money. If she has the capacity to make a major gift each year, she is probably asked to get involved with a wide variety of nonprofits. You have the advantage! This prospect is already involved in your congregation and has given you signs that she is ready to donate. This is not a cold call; this is an interactive, respectful conversation, where you will move the prospect to making or renewing a gift to this year's annual fund.

Is the Donor Ready to Be Asked?

The first step is to recognize when a prospective donor is ready to be asked. Signs vary, but may include that the prospective donor answers your phone calls, volunteers more, and/or makes gifts in kind. Because he is open to continuing the conversation about the positive and exciting aspects of the synagogue and will take the meeting, he is giving you signs that he is ready for the ask.

Making the Appointment

The second step in overcoming your anxiety is to obtain an appointment for a face-to-face meeting. The entire appointment-making process becomes much easier if you truly prepare for the call in great detail.

Here is a sure-fire way to "score" the appointment, which enhances your chance for success.

Begin by clarifying your objectives. Make sure that the "lead"— the first sentence or paragraph of your story—answers the classic journalist's questions: Who, what, when, where, why and how. (For more details, see page 126.)

Then write a script (not a monologue) for your side of the call. In that way you will be able to function in an unconsciously competent manner and be prepared to listen actively to the person on the other side of the conversation.

Does the Ask Have to Be Face-to-Face?

Yes. You will not raise as much money or learn enough about the donor to continue the conversation if you do it via email or over the phone. Both parties are less invested in a phone conversation than a personal meeting. And remember, this is about continued investment. If you start out shortchanging the interaction, you will never reach capacity.

Stage 4: Expanding the Circle—Leveraging the New Donor's Network

Once the commitment to make a gift has been secured, you enter the fourth stage, where you use your strengthened relationship with the donor to expand the circle. Now your new (or renewed) donor, whose enthusiasm is reinforced by your disciplined plan of stewardship, begins to introduce others to the process. This is the last step in the cycle, as donors get to bring people to a gateway event, just as they were engaged at the very beginning.

To succeed in this fourth stage, you must plan to help donors talk with their friends and introduce them to the congregation's annual fund.

The process begins with the first contact after the gift. Like the follow-up call after the initial gateway event, an immediate contact is essential. The call, which can be performed by the solicitor or someone else involved in the initial gateway event, allows you to let donors know right away how excited you are to receive their latest gift. Such a telephone call within two days of receiving the gift employs a basic follow-up call script including the one "killer" question:

Is there anyone you might want to invite to learn more about what we are doing?

You can expect that the conversation will be a positive one because donors feel good about their gift. They are happy to hear from you, and you are providing them with an opportunity to deepen their relationship with you and the synagogue.

You can explain that your task now is to engage other donors to expand the circle of supporters. You might start by asking this donor if she would like to host a gateway event and help you create an invitation list of prospective donors. She will expect you to treat her friends with the utmost care and respect. If you have followed each of the steps in the cycle, the donor will trust you to do for her friends and family what you did for her.

The dream for you and the congregation is that each new referral from one of your donors will also become a lifelong supporter. Thus, the circle grows exponentially in an ever-widening way, just like the ripples in the pond when you start with a single stone—one donor—who introduces two new donors, each of whom introduces two more.

Conclusion

This Is Not the End ... It Is But the Beginning

For us, this is the end of the book. For you, the reader, this is only the beginning. Hopefully you now have an understanding of what it will take to accomplish successful fundraising at your synagogue. You can achieve your dreams of financial stability, gather your volunteers and staff, and lead them to a new reality.

The future of your synagogue depends upon having the funds to fulfill the congregation's mission and achieve your vision. By overcoming your fears of asking for money, you can help others join in the incredible feeling that you are doing all that you can do for your congregation. When you eliminate those fears, funding for your current and future programs, for normal building maintenance, and for stabilizing your annual fund will all be assured. By following the plans outlined in this book, you will have reimagined a critical revenue stream for the congregation and laid the groundwork for a capital or endowment campaign in the future. And you are including your entire congregation in the process.

So we will leave you with one last piece of advice. Do not let this book sit on the shelf for years. Look at it holistically and start a methodical change, or pick it up once a month and decide what new piece you can incorporate into your work. Either way, start now. Ask the hard questions of your colleagues, and encourage them to challenge you back. Changing your current practices will not always be easy, but the rewards for your congregation will include a financial sustainability that previously seemed unimaginable. And that will build community and help you thrive for years to come.

Acknowledgments

We should start by acknowledging Stuart M. Matlins, publisher of Jewish Lights and David's friend of long standing, who called with an idea about a book based on the newsletter that our firm, Mersky, Jaffe & Associates, has published for more than a decade. Stuart has been a subscriber from its earliest days. The newsletter—initially monthly, now weekly—has been largely written and edited by Abigail, along with monthly pieces from David and additional help from some of the firm's associates.

Stuart said to us—both on the phone and then at a wonderful day in the offices of Jewish Lights Publishing—that we had great content that we had published and we should gather it in a book for the synagogue world. He said there was an increasing need for congregations to connect with their members in a relational way as opposed to the transactional and consumerist mindset with which most people view affiliation today. His essential question was "How can congregations develop the philanthropic and financial resources essential to achieve the vision of a twenty-first-century synagogue as a center of engagement and enrichment of Jewish life?"

Stuart said it would be easy … we had all the content; we only needed to repurpose it. So, greatly flattered, we began the task of "repurposing," expanding upon brief articles and creating new material to share what we had learned in our many years of counseling congregations throughout North America. The result of those labors—and the improvements made by the great team at Jewish Lights Publishing (including Emily Wichland, Tim Holtz, Leah Brewer, and Rachel Shields) is what you now hold in your hand (or view on your screen). Anything that you find good and valuable is a credit to those who have taught us throughout the years: our teachers, clients, family, and friends. Any errors are our responsibility alone.

As you work your way through the book and implement the programs and processes we recommend, we welcome any feedback that you would care to offer by emailing us at info@merskyjaffe.com. We hope that this book helps you create community, respond to the aspirations of those who affiliate with your congregation, and enhance the respect you have for the diversity and individuality of each and every donor. We also hope you will learn that a creative program of development and fundraising will draw people ever closer to the congregation as a community of funders and will strengthen their engagement. And, above all, we hope that you will now be able to feel confident on the path to financial sustainability for your congregation and that you have a core group of funders who are not afraid to ask their fellow congregants to join them in supporting your community's vision and mission.

For Carol, with whom I walk through life.

—David

And for Adam, Moriah, and Isabel—thank you for your love and support.

—Abigail

Appendix 1
Donor Recognition Policy

Since the third century, when the first mosaic inscriptions on ancient buildings were uncovered, it has been a practice to give recognition to those who have helped make construction possible. This tradition continued throughout the Middle Ages until modern times in the form of wall inscriptions and donor plaques.

This tradition developed because it encouraged donors to be as generous as possible in support of their community and served as a model for future generations to emulate. Appropriate donor recognition has become integral to the philanthropic world because it works and is a way to offer donors appropriate thanks for their material support.

Specific categories of giving are as follows:

Amount of Gift	Hebrew Name*	English Name
$100,000+	מיסדים M'yas'dim	Founders
$50,000 to $99,999	מקימים M'kayy'mim	Sustainers
$25,000 to $49,999	בונים Bonim	Builders
$10,000 to $24,999	נדבונים N'dvonim	Benefactors
$5,000 to $9,999	פטרונים Patronim	Patrons
$2,500 to $4,999	ידידים Yedidim	Friends
$1,000 to $2,499	תורמים Tor'mim	Donors
Gifts of less than $1,000	נותנים Not'nim	Contributors

* It is not intended that the Hebrew be transliterated, but rather it should be shown in print and on a donor wall in unvocalized Hebrew characters only.

In keeping with this tradition, the board of directors of Congregation Emanuel, upon the recommendation of its development committee, adopts the following donor recognition policy:

1. Donor recognition will be done in a way that displays the generosity of our donors while retaining the aesthetic of our space.
2. Donors will specify how their names will be listed.
3. Donors will be grouped by named recognition category. No numerical categories will be used anywhere in such recognition. Within each recognition category, names will be arranged by alphabetical order of last names. If a donor family uses two last names, the donor family will decide which name goes first.
4. Any variations or exceptions to these policies, consistent with the spirit and intent of the policies, can be made by unanimous approval of the development committee, along with the solicitor of the gift (if the solicitor is different from any of the aforementioned). If unanimous approval of this committee cannot be achieved, any two members of the committee can refer the matter to the board of directors for consideration and a vote. No variations or exceptions to this policy may be promised to any donor until after a decision has been made consistent with this paragraph.

In addition, capital campaign donor recognition policies should include:

1. Donors may designate their gifts for particular spaces or items and will receive recognition linking their gifts to those spaces or items. For example, a gift of a classroom will be designated with a proximate visual recognition of the donor's name and, if otherwise consistent with this policy, with the name(s) of the individual(s) honored or remembered by the gift.
2. The levels of giving entitling donors to designate spaces or items ("the pricing") will be established based on the judgment of the development committee and the board.
3. Donors will be given visual recognition after the first payment of the pledge has been received or an irrevocable charitable gift contract has been executed.

Appendix 2
Major Gifts Moves Management Worksheets

The chief characteristics of a robust major gifts moves management process are discipline and accountability. What follows is a system to achieve outstanding results in identifying, gathering information about, and engaging with prospective donors; cultivating relationships; soliciting gifts; and stewarding the ongoing connection with the congregation.

The system of moves management begins with the identification of a prospective donor. The following data and answers to the questions need to be completed in order for the prospect to be added to the major-gifts management list. All this information should be entered into the synagogue's data management system so that it can be easily retrieved.

Major Gifts Moves Management Prospect Identification

Date:_____

Prospect Name:	Spouse Name:
Address:	Telephone:

1. Why is this individual a prospect? In what areas of synagogue life has this individual expressed a particular interest? For what purposes should funding be sought?

_____
_____
_____
_____

2. At what level do you consider this individual capable of giving?

☐ $1,000–2,499   ☐ $2,500–4,999   ☐ $5,000–9,999   ☐ $10,000+

3. What is your present relationship with this individual? Has there been any contact with this prospect? Are there staff or volunteers who may provide information and assistance?

_____
_____
_____
_____

4. Who should be assigned as the prospect manager for this individual? Explain.

_____
_____
_____
_____

5. What is the planned next move with regard to this prospect? What is the plan for the next six to twelve months?

_____
_____
_____
_____

Submitted by:_____   Title:_____

Major Gifts Moves Management Prospect Review Form

Name: _____

Date: _____

Name of Prospect	City, State	I know this prospect very well	I can share information about this prospect	I have access to this prospect	Comments

Major Gifts Moves Management Call Report

Contact Name(s): _____

_____

Date of Call: _____ Name of Person Making Call: _____

Type of Call: ☐ Phone ☐ In Person

Location of Personal Visit: ☐ Home ☐ Office ☐ On-Site ☐ Other: _____

Purpose of Call: ☐ Cultivation ☐ Solicitation ☐ Other

Summary of Call: _____

_____

_____

_____

_____

If assigned as prospect manager, please indicate plan and next step	Next Step
☐ Continue cultivation	
☐ Remove from PM list	
☐ Reassign to other PM	

Submitted by: _____ Title: _____

Please submit address changes on reverse and check here ☐

Major Gifts Moves Management Weekly Summary

Prospect Manager: _____

Date: _____

Prospect Name and ID Number	$ Rating	Target Ask	Pipeline Status*	Date of Last Contact	Nature of Contact	Date of Next Contact	Next Step	Comments

Submitted by: _____

* Identification—10% Information—25% Interest—50% Involvement—75% Investment—100% (see step 5 of "Creating a Moves Management Strategy," page 152)

Major Gifts Moves Management Dashboard

Date: _____

Total Number of Prospects in the System: _____

Total Number of Assigned Prospects: _____

Solicitor Names	Natalie	Jordan	Liz	Eli
Number of gifts				
Amount pledged				
Rated dollar value of prospects and donors				
Number of assigned prospects				
Number of prospect emails				
Number of prospect phone calls				
Number of prospect meetings				
Total prospect contacts				
Number of assigned donors				
Number of donor calls				
Number of donor emails				
Number of donor meetings				
Total donor "touches"				
Total contacts				

Glossary

80/20 rule The generally accepted theory, first identified by the nineteenth-century Italian economist Vilfredo Pareto, that 80 percent of your fundraising revenue will come from 20 percent of your donors. The 80/20 rule is a way to segment donors for both annual and capital campaigns.

acknowledge To express thanks for a gift; may be in written or oral form, communicated privately or publicly.

acknowledgment letter A letter used to thank a donor for a contribution.

active phase *(or public phase)* The general solicitation of a community of donors during a capital or endowment campaign; usually follows the successful completion of a campaign's quiet phase.

advance gift *(or initial gift)* A donation given early in a campaign that demonstrates a commitment to a campaign and creates momentum for the quiet phase.

advisory committee *(or advisory board)* An influential and experienced group that offers counsel, financial resources, and prestige to a nonprofit or cause with which it is associated.

allocated costs Indirect expenses, such as management supervision, occupancy, and development costs for all programs.

annual giving An amount given each year to a nonprofit or a fundraising program that develops support on a yearly basis.

anonymous gift A donation that is not attributed to a donor in any public way.

appreciated security A security, such as a stock or bond greater than the cost basis.

board *(also known as trustees, governing board, and/or board of directors)* The fiscal, policy, and strategic governing body of a nonprofit organization.

board member A person who serves on a governing or advisory board.

campaign analysis A comprehensive report that includes an overview of prospective income, projected expenses, the number and size of current gifts, and any qualitative data that can help provide an understanding of the campaign.

campaign brochure A document that summarizes the case for the campaign as well as the vision and aspirations the congregation hopes to achieve through the successful completion of the fundraising. Sometimes referred to as a "leave-behind."

campaign chair The lead volunteer of a campaign, charged with guiding, energizing, and motivating the entire volunteer team as well as the staff.

campaign of one The process of personalizing both strategic and tactical means to engage a single donor.

campaign support staff Paid personnel who fulfill functions as diverse as bookkeeping, record keeping, researching, coordinating meetings, and offering general support for the campaign.

capital campaign A focused fundraising effort for a building, endowment, or some combination of the two, designed to reach a predetermined financial goal within a specific time frame.

case statement A document that clearly explains and inspires a prospect to donate to your congregation for this campaign. Additional explanation of a case statement can be found in chapter 9, "The Case for Giving."

cause-related marketing *(or cause marketing)* A type of marketing that combines the efforts of a nonprofit and a for-profit business to promote a product or service that will benefit both organizations.

challenge gift *(or matching gift)* A gift donated with conditions as a way to encourage others to give.

charitable deduction A gift given to a 501(c)(3) charity that is deductible from income tax or estate tax.

community foundation A nonprofit organization for individuals and families who choose to practice their philanthropy through a private foundation.

corporate foundation A private foundation arm of a for-profit corporation that provides grants according to preestablished guidelines.

cultivation Promoting and growing a donor or prospect's involvement with a congregation.

cultivation event A special event to introduce a prospect to a synagogue and its work.

deferred gift A gift (such as a bequest, a life insurance policy, a charitable remainder trust, or a gift annuity) that is committed to a charitable organization but is not available for use until some future time, usually upon the death of the donor.

designated gift *(or restricted gift)* A donation with temporary or permanent restrictions as to how and when the funds can be used.

development The process that manages relationships between and among donors and the organization.

development audit An objective assessment of your congregation that examines the strengths and weaknesses of your development efforts as well as the opportunities and threats in the environment in which it seeks resources.

development consultant A skilled professional engaged to give advice and services related to development and fundraising.

development consulting firm *(or fundraising counsel)* A firm engaged to provide nonprofits with advice surrounding fundraising and development functions.

donor acquisition The disciplined plan to identify and acquire new donors.

donor list A compilation of donors who have given to a nonprofit, often to provide recognition.

donor recognition The congregation's way of acknowledging and recognizing a donor, which may be in letters, public listings, private parties, and/or other applicable means of citing the donor's generosity.

easy-to-access research *(also known as internal prospect research)* Qualitative and quantitative data about a person that is easy to discover with minimal effort.

endowment A restricted fund created to provide revenue for a purpose determined when the principal is provided to the nonprofit, like a synagogue.

face-to-face solicitation *(or personal solicitation)* The in-person meeting between a solicitor and a prospective donor during which the donor is asked for a gift or pledge.

fact sheet An overview of a nonprofit, like a synagogue, that may include the mission, vision, revenue and expenses, number of participants in various programs and services, and other information.

family foundation A private foundation, frequently unstaffed, that is created as a giving vehicle for one or more family members to perpetuate the family's values and philanthropic agenda.

feasibility study A survey of community leaders, through confidential, one-on-one interviews, focus groups, and online surveys, to test a case for giving as well as whether and to what degree the community will support a proposed capital or endowment campaign.

feasibility study report The results of a feasibility study, with anonymous verbatim quotations, that will help develop realistic, targeted fundraising objectives.

founders' syndrome A condition seen in nonprofits in which one or more founders continue to exert great influence to inhibit changes that could help grow and improve the organization.

gift-acceptance policy The list of protocols, as guided by the nonprofit's internal guidelines as well as local and federal law, to determine which types of gifts will be accepted.

gift chart *(also known as a gift table or gift pyramid)* A chart that indicates the required number of prospects who become donors at each level of giving to achieve the desired goal.

gift in kind A donation of goods or services instead of a financial contribution.

identification Finding prospects for your fundraising and/or board development process.

initial gift See *advance gift*.

in-kind donations See *gift in kind*.

lapsed donor A donor who has made a donation in previous years but not in the current fiscal year. Lapsed donors are often referred to as LYBUNTs, PYBUNTs, and/or SYBUNTs, which are acronyms for Last/Previous/Past Year/Sometime But Unfortunately Not This Year (the Y is silent).

lay leadership Volunteer leaders in a congregational setting use this term to differentiate themselves from the staff or clergy who serve as leaders.

life-income gift An irrevocable transfer of property to a nonprofit in which the donor, and possibly another beneficiary, retains an income interest.

meaningful gift A donation to a nonprofit, such as a synagogue, achievable within your budget but requires you to stop and think if that is the right amount, and will give you the knowledge that you truly did all that you could do financially to help the organization.

moves management A process in which you take a series of steps (moves) for and with an identified prospect designed to prompt the individual prospect to action—"moving" toward the next gift.

philanthropic investment Charitable giving based on the donor's belief that your organization is worthy of his time, energy, and donations.

planned giving A process to support a nonprofit, like a synagogue, through bequests, charitable gift annuities, charitable remainder trusts, and charitable lead trusts.

prospect Any potential donor who has been identified as someone who may give to the congregation.

prospect list An inventory of individuals who have been chosen as potential donors.

prospect profile The collective information about a prospective donor; may include demographic and family information, financial data, giving history, special interests, and connections to the nonprofit whether based on mission or personal relationships.

prospect research The in-depth search for relevant, publicly available information on prospective donors. Chapter 8 explains what prospect research can tell you.

rating The process by which prospective donors are placed into likely giving categories.

relationship manager The person who will set up meetings, submit notes, follow up, and create next steps for a prospect or donor.

segment To create donor and/or prospect groups for research, rating, engagement, and solicitation.

stewardship The series of activities and events that take place after a gift, in order to ensure a satisfied donor as well as a repeat donor.

strategic plan The examination of a congregation's goals and objectives to determine where you are, where you're going, and the best route to get there.

stretch gift A donation that reaches a donor's capacity to give as well as a gift beyond what the donor could have imagined she would make.

sustaining gifts *(also known as recurring gifts or monthly giving)* A donor's commitment to a monthly contribution. These gifts are most often paid via a credit or debit card with no end date.

token gift A gift that is easily given by a donor and is considerably below capacity.

touch A cultivation or stewardship move that connects with a donor and the donor's interests. Examples of how to "touch" a donor can be found in chapter 14.

unrestricted gift A donation offered without restrictions, to be used at the congregation's discretion.

volunteer leadership The people who work without financial compensation to help bring the dreams and visions of the community to reality.

Bible Study / Midrash

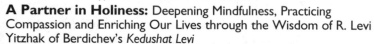

Passing Life's Tests: Spiritual Reflections on the Trial of Abraham, the Binding of Isaac *By Rabbi Bradley Shavit Artson, DHL*
Invites us to use this powerful tale as a tool for our own soul wrestling, to confront our existential sacrifices and enable us to face—and surmount—life's tests.
6 × 9, 176 pp, Quality PB, 978-1-58023-631-7 **$18.99**

Speaking Torah: Spiritual Teachings from around the Maggid's Table—in Two Volumes *By Arthur Green, with Ebn Leader, Ariel Evan Mayse and Or N. Rose*
The most powerful Hasidic teachings made accessible—from some of the world's preeminent authorities on Jewish thought and spirituality.
Volume 1—6 × 9, 512 pp, HC, 978-1-58023-668-3 **$34.99**
Volume 2—6 × 9, 448 pp, HC, 978-1-58023-694-2 **$34.99**

A Partner in Holiness: Deepening Mindfulness, Practicing Compassion and Enriching Our Lives through the Wisdom of R. Levi Yitzhak of Berdichev's *Kedushat Levi*
By Rabbi Jonathan P. Slater, DMin; Foreword by Arthur Green; Preface by Rabby Nancy Flam
Contemporary mindfulness and classical Hasidic spirituality are brought together to inspire a satisfying spiritual life of practice.
Volume 1—6 × 9, 336 pp, HC, 978-1-58023-794-9 **$35.00**
Volume 2—6 × 9, 288 pp, HC, 978-1-58023-795-6 **$35.00**

The Genesis of Leadership: What the Bible Teaches Us about Vision, Values and Leading Change *By Rabbi Nathan Laufer; Foreword by Senator Joseph I. Lieberman*
6 × 9, 288 pp, Quality PB, 978-1-58023-352-1 **$18.99**

Hineini in Our Lives: Learning How to Respond to Others through 14 Biblical Texts and Personal Stories *By Dr. Norman J. Cohen* 6 × 9, 240 pp, Quality PB, 978-1-58023-274-6 **$18.99**

Masking and Unmasking Ourselves: Interpreting Biblical Texts on Clothing & Identity *By Dr. Norman J. Cohen* 6 × 9, 224 pp, HC, 978-1-58023-461-0 **$24.99**
Quality PB, 978-1-58023-839-7 **$18.99**

The Messiah and the Jews: Three Thousand Years of Tradition, Belief and Hope *By Rabbi Elaine Rose Glickman; Foreword by Rabbi Neil Gillman, PhD*
Preface by Rabbi Judith Z. Abrams, PhD 6 × 9, 192 pp, Quality PB, 978-1-58023-690-4 **$16.99**

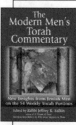

The Modern Men's Torah Commentary: New Insights from Jewish Men on the 54 Weekly Torah Portions *Edited by Rabbi Jeffrey K. Salkin*
6 × 9, 368 pp, HC, 978-1-58023-395-8 **$24.99**

Moses and the Journey to Leadership: Timeless Lessons of Effective Management from the Bible and Today's Leaders *By Dr. Norman J. Cohen*
6 × 9, 240 pp, Quality PB, 978-1-58023-351-4 **$18.99**; HC, 978-1-58023-227-2 **$21.99**

The Other Talmud—The *Yerushalmi*: Unlocking the Secrets of *The Talmud of Israel* for Judaism Today *By Rabbi Judith Z. Abrams, PhD*
6 × 9, 256 pp, HC, 978-1-58023-463-4 **$24.99**

Sage Tales: Wisdom and Wonder from the Rabbis of the Talmud
By Rabbi Burton L. Visotzky
6 × 9, 256 pp, Quality PB, 978-1-58023-791-8 **$19.99**; HC, 978-1-58023-456-6 **$24.99**

The Torah Revolution: Fourteen Truths That Changed the World
By Rabbi Reuven Hammer, PhD 6 × 9, 240 pp, Quality PB, 978-1-58023-789-5 **$18.99**
HC, 978-1-58023-457-3 **$24.99**

The Wisdom of Judaism: An Introduction to the Values of the Talmud
By Rabbi Dov Peretz Elkins 6 × 9, 192 pp, Quality PB, 978-1-58023-327-9 **$16.99**

Or phone, fax, mail or email to: **JEWISH LIGHTS** Publishing
Sunset Farm Offices, Route 4 • P.O. Box 237 • Woodstock, Vermont 05091
Tel: (802) 457-4000 • Fax: (802) 457-4004 • www.jewishlights.com
Credit card orders: **(800) 962-4544** (8:30AM–5:30PM EST Monday–Friday)
Generous discounts on quantity orders. SATISFACTION GUARANTEED. Prices subject to change.

Children's Books by Sandy Eisenberg Sasso

The *Shema* in the Mezuzah
Listening to Each Other
Introduces children ages 3 to 6 to the words of the *Shema* and the custom of putting up the mezuzah. Winner, National Jewish Book Award.
9 x 12, 32 pp, Full-color illus., HC, 978-1-58023-506-8 **$18.99** *For ages 3–6*

Adam & Eve's First Sunset
God's New Day
Explores fear and hope, faith and gratitude in ways that will delight kids and adults—inspiring us to bless each of God's days and nights.
9 x 12, 32 pp, Full-color illus., HC, 978-1-58023-177-0 **$17.95** *For ages 4 & up*

Also Available as a Board Book: **Adam and Eve's New Day**
5 x 5, 24 pp, Full-color illus., Board Book, 978-1-59473-205-8 **$7.99*** *For ages 1–4*

But God Remembered
Stories of Women from Creation to the Promised Land
Four different stories of women—Lilith, Serach, Bityah and the Daughters of Z—teach us important values through their faith and actions.
9 x 12, 32 pp, Full-color illus., Quality PB, 978-1-58023-372-9 **$8.99** *For ages 8 & up*

For Heaven's Sake
Heaven is often found where you least expect it.
9 x 12, 32 pp, Full-color illus., HC, 978-1-58023-054-4 **$16.95** *For ages 4 & up*

God Said Amen
An inspiring story about hearing the answers to our prayers.
9 x 12, 32 pp, Full-color illus., HC, 978-1-58023-080-3 **$16.95** *For ages 4 & up*

God's Paintbrush: Special 10th Anniversary Edition
Wonderfully interactive, invites children of all faiths and backgrounds to encounter God through moments in their own lives. Provides questions adult and child can explore together. 11 x 8¼, 32 pp, Full-color illus., HC, 978-1-58023-195-4 **$18.99** *For ages 4 & up*

Also Available as a Board Book: **I Am God's Paintbrush**
5 x 5, 24 pp, Full-color illus., Board Book, 978-1-59473-265-2 **$7.99*** *For ages 1–4*

Also Available: **God's Paintbrush Teacher's Guide**
8½ x 11, 32 pp, PB, 978-1-879045-57-6 **$8.95**

God's Paintbrush Celebration Kit
A Spiritual Activity Kit for Teachers and Students of All Faiths, All Backgrounds
9½ x 12, 40 Full-color Activity Sheets & Teacher Folder w/ complete instructions
HC, 978-1-58023-050-6 **$21.95**
8-Student Activity Sheet Pack (40 sheets/5 sessions), 978-1-58023-058-2 **$19.95**
Single-Student Activity Sheet Pack (5 sessions), 978-1-58023-059-9 **$3.95**

In God's Name
Like an ancient myth in its poetic text and vibrant illustrations, this award-winning modern fable about the search for God's name celebrates the diversity and, at the same time, the unity of all people.
9 x 12, 32 pp, Full-color illus., HC, 978-1-879045-26-2 **$18.99** *For ages 4 & up*

Also Available as a Board Book: **What Is God's Name?**
5 x 5, 24 pp, Full-color illus., Board Book, 978-1-893361-10-2 **$8.99*** *For ages 1–4*

Also Available in Spanish: **El nombre de Dios**
9 x 12, 32 pp, Full-color illus., HC, 978-1-893361-63-8 **$16.95** *For ages 4 & up*

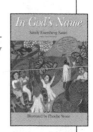

Noah's Wife
The Story of Naamah
When God tells Noah to bring the animals of the world onto the ark, God also calls on Naamah, Noah's wife, to save each plant on earth.
9 x 12, 32 pp, Full-color illus., HC, 978-1-58023-134-3 **$16.95** *For ages 4 & up*

Also Available as a Board Book: **Naamah, Noah's Wife**
5 x 5, 24 pp, Full-color illus., Board Book, 978-1-893361-56-0 **$7.95*** *For ages 1–4*

**A book from SkyLight Paths, Jewish Lights' sister imprint*

Theology / Philosophy

Renewing the Process of Creation: A Jewish Integration of Science and Spirit *By Rabbi Bradley Shavit Artson, DHL*
A daring blend of Jewish theology, science and Process Thought, exploring personal actions through Judaism and the sciences as dynamically interactive and mutually informative. 6 x 9, 208 pp, HC, 978-1-58023-833-5 **$24.99**

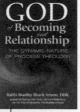

Does the Soul Survive? 2nd Edition: A Jewish Journey to Belief in Afterlife, Past Lives & Living with Purpose *By Rabbi Elie Kaplan Spitz*
Foreword by Brian L. Weiss, MD A skeptic turned believer recounts his quest to uncover the Jewish tradition's answers about what happens to our souls after death.
6 x 9, 288 pp, Quality PB, 978-1-58023-818-2 **$18.99**

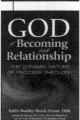

God of Becoming and Relationship: The Dynamic Nature of Process Theology *By Rabbi Bradley Shavit Artson, DHL* Explains how Process Theology breaks us free from the strictures of ancient Greek and medieval European philosophy. 6 x 9, 208 pp, HC, 978-1-58023-713-0 **$24.99**

The Way of Man: According to Hasidic Teaching
By Martin Buber; New Translation and Introduction by Rabbi Bernard H. Mehlman and Dr. Gabriel E. Padawer; Foreword by Paul Mendes-Flohr
An accessible and engaging new translation of Buber's classic work—*available as an eBook only.* eBook, 978-1-58023-601-0 **$18.99**

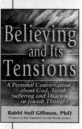

Believing and Its Tensions: A Personal Conversation about God, Torah, Suffering and Death in Jewish Thought *By Rabbi Neil Gillman, PhD*
5½ x 8½, 144 pp, HC, 978-1-58023-669-0 **$19.99**

The Death of Death: Resurrection and Immortality in Jewish Thought
By Rabbi Neil Gillman, PhD 6 x 9, 336 pp, Quality PB, 978-1-58023-081-0 **$19.99**

From Defender to Critic: The Search for a New Jewish Self
By Dr. David Hartman (z"l) 6 x 9, 336 pp, HC, 978-1-58023-515-0 **$35.00**

The God Who Hates Lies: Confronting & Rethinking Jewish Tradition
By Dr. David Hartman (z"l) with Charlie Buckholtz 6 x 9, 208 pp, Quality PB, 978-1-58023-790-1 **$19.99**

A Heart of Many Rooms: Celebrating the Many Voices within Judaism
By Dr. David Hartman (z"l) 6 x 9, 352 pp, Quality PB, 978-1-58023-156-5 **$24.99**

Jewish Theology in Our Time: A New Generation Explores the Foundations and Future of Jewish Belief *Edited by Rabbi Elliot J. Cosgrove, PhD; Foreword by Rabbi David J. Wolpe Preface by Rabbi Carole B. Balin, PhD*
6 x 9, 240 pp, Quality PB, 978-1-58023-630-0 **$19.99**; HC, 978-1-58023-413-9 **$24.99**

Maimonides—Essential Teachings on Jewish Faith & Ethics: The Book of Knowledge & the Thirteen Principles of Faith—Annotated & Explained
Translation and Annotation by Rabbi Marc D. Angel, PhD
5½ x 8½, 224 pp, Quality PB, 978-1-59473-311-6 **$18.99***

Our Religious Brains: What Cognitive Science Reveals about Belief, Mortality, Community and Our Relationship with God *By Rabbi Ralph D. Mecklenburger; Foreword by Dr. Howard Kelfer; Preface by Dr. Neil Gillman*
6 x 9, 224 pp, HC, 978-1-58023-508-2 **$24.99**; Quality PB, 978-1-58023-840-3 **$18.99**

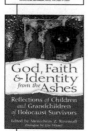

God, Faith & Identity from the Ashes
Reflections of Children and Grandchildren of Holocaust Survivors
Almost ninety contributors from sixteen countries inform, challenge and inspire people of all backgrounds. *Edited by Menachem Z. Rosensaft; Prologue by Elie Wiesel*
6 x 9, 352 pp, HC, 978-1-58023-805-2 **$25.00**

I Am Jewish
Personal Reflections Inspired by the Last Words of Daniel Pearl
Almost 150 Jews—both famous and not—from all walks of life, from all around the world, write about many aspects of their Judaism.
Edited by Judea and Ruth Pearl 6 x 9, 304 pp, Deluxe PB w/ flaps, 978-1-58023-259-3 **$19.99**
Download a free copy of the *I Am Jewish Teacher's Guide* at www.jewishlights.com.

**A book from SkyLight Paths, Jewish Lights' sister imprint*

Life Cycle
Marriage / Parenting / Family / Aging

Jewish Spiritual Parenting: Wisdom, Activities, Rituals and Prayers for Raising Children with Spiritual Balance and Emotional Wholeness
By Rabbi Paul Kipnes and Michelle November, MSSW
Offers parents, grandparents, teachers and anyone who interacts with children creative first steps and next steps to make the Jewish holidays and every day engaging and inspiring. 6 x 9, 224 pp, Quality PB, 978-1-58023-821-2 **$18.99**

Jewish Wisdom for Growing Older: Finding Your Grit & Grace Beyond Midlife *By Rabbi Dayle A. Friedman, MSW, MA, BCC* Mines ancient Jewish wisdom for values, tools and precedents to embrace new opportunities and beginnings, shifting family roles and experiences of illness and death.
6 x 9, 176 pp, Quality PB, 978-1-58023-819-9 **$16.99**

Ethical Wills & How to Prepare Them
A Guide to Sharing Your Values from Generation to Generation
Edited by Rabbi Jack Riemer and Dr. Nathaniel Stampfer; Foreword by Rabbi Harold S. Kushner
A unique combination of "what is" and "how to" with examples of ethical wills and a step-by-step process that shows you how to prepare your own.
6 x 9, 272 pp, Quality PB, 978-1-58023-827-4 **$18.99**

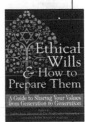

Secrets of a Soulful Marriage: Creating & Sustaining a Loving, Sacred Relationship *By Jim Sharon, EdD, and Ruth Sharon, MS*
Useful perspectives, tools and practices for cultivating a relationship; with insights from psychology, the wisdom of spiritual traditions and the experiences of many kinds of committed couples. 6 x 9, 192 pp, Quality PB, 978-1-59473-554-7 **$16.99***

Celebrating Your New Jewish Daughter: Creating Jewish Ways to Welcome Baby Girls into the Covenant—New and Traditional Ceremonies *By Debra Nussbaum Cohen*
Foreword by Rabbi Sandy Eisenberg Sasso 6 x 9, 272 pp, Quality PB, 978-1-58023-090-2 **$18.95**

The Creative Jewish Wedding Book, 2nd Edition: A Hands-On Guide to New & Old Traditions, Ceremonies & Celebrations *By Gabrielle Kaplan-Mayer*
9 x 9, 288 pp, b/w photos, Quality PB, 978-1-58023-398-9 **$19.99**

Divorce Is a Mitzvah: A Practical Guide to Finding Wholeness and Holiness When Your Marriage Dies *By Rabbi Perry Netter; Afterword by Rabbi Laura Geller*
6 x 9, 224 pp, Quality PB, 978-1-58023-172-5 **$18.99**

Embracing the Covenant: Converts to Judaism Talk About Why & How
By Rabbi Allan Berkowitz and Patti Moskovitz 6 x 9, 192 pp, Quality PB, 978-1-879045-50-7 **$18.99**

The Jewish Pregnancy Book: A Resource for the Soul, Body & Mind during Pregnancy, Birth & the First Three Months
By Sandy Falk, MD, and Rabbi Daniel Judson, with Steven A. Rapp
7 x 10, 208 pp, b/w photos, Quality PB, 978-1-58023-178-7 **$16.95**

Jewish Visions for Aging: A Professional Guide for Fostering Wholeness
By Rabbi Dale A. Friedman, MSW, MAJCS, BCC; Foreword by Thomas R. Cole, PhD
Preface by Dr. Eugene B. Borowitz 6 x 9, 272 pp, HC, 978-1-58023-348-4 **$24.99**

Making a Successful Jewish Interfaith Marriage: The Big Tent Judaism Guide to Opportunities, Challenges and Resources *By Rabbi Kerry M. Olitzky with Joan Peterson Littman*
6 x 9, 176 pp, Quality PB, 978-1-58023-170-1 **$18.99**

A Man's Responsibility: A Jewish Guide to Being a Son, a Partner in Marriage, a Father and a Community Leader *By Rabbi Joseph B. Meszler*
6 x 9, 192 pp, Quality PB, 978-1-58023-435-1 **$16.99**

The New Jewish Baby Album: Creating and Celebrating the Beginning of a Spiritual Life—A Jewish Lights Companion
By the Editors at Jewish Lights; Foreword by Anita Diamant; Preface by Rabbi Sandy Eisenberg Sasso
8 x 10, 64 pp, Deluxe Padded HC, Full-color illus., 978-1-58023-138-1 **$19.95**

The New Jewish Baby Book, 2nd Edition: Names, Ceremonies & Customs—A Guide for Today's Families *By Anita Diamant* 6 x 9, 320 pp, Quality PB, 978-1-58023-251-7 **$19.99**

Parenting Jewish Teens: A Guide for the Perplexed
By Joanne Doades 6 x 9, 176 pp, Quality PB, 978-1-58023-305-7 **$16.99**

*A book from SkyLight Paths, Jewish Lights' sister imprint

Ecology / Environment

A Wild Faith: Jewish Ways into Wilderness, Wilderness Ways into Judaism
By Rabbi Mike Comins; Foreword by Nigel Savage
6 x 9, 240 pp, Quality PB, 978-1-58023-316-3 **$18.99**

Ecology & the Jewish Spirit: Where Nature & the Sacred Meet
Edited by Ellen Bernstein 6 x 9, 288 pp, Quality PB, 978-1-58023-082-7 **$18.99**

Torah of the Earth: Exploring 4,000 Years of Ecology in Jewish Thought
Vol. 1: Biblical Israel & Rabbinic Judaism; Vol. 2: Zionism & Eco-Judaism
Edited by Rabbi Arthur Waskow Vol. 1. 6 x 9, 272 pp, Quality PB, 978-1-58023-086-5 **$19.95**
Vol. 2. 6 x 9, 336 pp, Quality PB, 978-1-58023-087-2 **$19.95**

The Way Into Judaism and the Environment *By Jeremy Benstein, PhD*
6 x 9, 288 pp, Quality PB, 978-1-58023-368-2 **$18.99**; HC, 978-1-58023-268-5 **$24.99**

Graphic Novels / Graphic History

The Adventures of Rabbi Harvey: A Graphic Novel of Jewish Wisdom and Wit in the
Wild West *By Steve Sheinkin*
6 x 9, 144 pp, Full-color illus., Quality PB, 978-1-58023-310-1 **$16.99**

Rabbi Harvey Rides Again: A Graphic Novel of Jewish Folktales Let Loose in the
Wild West *By Steve Sheinkin*
6 x 9, 144 pp, Full-color illus., Quality PB, 978-1-58023-347-7 **$16.99**

Rabbi Harvey vs. the Wisdom Kid: A Graphic Novel of Dueling Jewish Folktales in
the Wild West *By Steve Sheinkin*
6 x 9, 144 pp, Full-color illus., Quality PB, 978-1-58023-422-1 **$16.99**

The Story of the Jews: A 4,000-Year Adventure—A Graphic History Book
By Stan Mack 6 x 9, 304 pp, Illus., Quality PB, 978-1-58023-155-8 **$18.99**

Grief / Healing

Facing Illness, Finding God: How Judaism Can Help You and Caregivers Cope
When Body or Spirit Fails *By Rabbi Joseph B. Meszler*
6 x 9, 208 pp, Quality PB, 978-1-58023-423-8 **$16.99**

Grief in Our Seasons: A Mourner's Kaddish Companion *By Rabbi Kerry M. Olitzky*
4½ x 6½, 448 pp, Quality PB, 978-1-879045-55-2 **$18.99**

Healing and the Jewish Imagination: Spiritual and Practical Perspectives on
Judaism and Health *Edited by Rabbi William Cutter, PhD*
6 x 9, 240 pp, Quality PB, 978-1-58023-373-6 **$19.99**

Healing from Despair: Choosing Wholeness in a Broken World
By Rabbi Elie Kaplan Spitz with Erica Shapiro Taylor; Foreword by Abraham J. Twerski, MD
5½ x 8½, 208 pp, Quality PB, 978-1-58023-436-8 **$16.99**

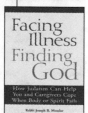

Healing of Soul, Healing of Body: Spiritual Leaders Unfold the Strength & Solace
in Psalms *Edited by Rabbi Simkha Y. Weintraub, LCSW*
6 x 9, 128 pp, 2-color illus. text, Quality PB, 978-1-879045-31-6 **$16.99**

Judaism and Health: A Handbook of Practical, Professional and Scholarly Resources
Edited by Jeff Levin, PhD, MPH, and Michele F. Prince, LCSW, MAJCS
Foreword by Rabbi Elliot N. Dorff, PhD 6 x 9, 448 pp, HC, 978-1-58023-714-7 **$50.00**

Midrash & Medicine: Healing Body and Soul in the Jewish Interpretive Tradition
Edited by Rabbi William Cutter, PhD; Foreword by Michele F. Prince, LCSW, MAJCS
6 x 9, 352 pp, Quality PB, 978-1-58023-484-9 **$21.99**

Mourning & Mitzvah, 2nd Edition: A Guided Journal for Walking the Mourner's
Path through Grief to Healing *By Rabbi Anne Brener, LCSW*
7½ x 9, 304 pp, Quality PB, 978-1-58023-113-8 **$19.99**

Tears of Sorrow, Seeds of Hope, 2nd Edition: A Jewish Spiritual Companion
for Infertility and Pregnancy Loss *By Rabbi Nina Beth Cardin*
6 x 9, 208 pp, Quality PB, 978-1-58023-233-3 **$18.99**

A Time to Mourn, a Time to Comfort, 2nd Edition:
A Guide to Jewish Bereavement *By Dr. Ron Wolfson; Foreword by Rabbi David J. Wolpe*
7 x 9, 384 pp, Quality PB, 978-1-58023-253-1 **$21.99**

When a Grandparent Dies: A Kid's Own Remembering Workbook for Dealing
with Shiva and the Year Beyond *By Nechama Liss-Levinson, PhD*
8 x 10, 48 pp, 2-color text, HC, 978-1-879045-44-6 **$15.95** *For ages 7–13*

Meditation / Yoga

Increasing Wholeness: Jewish Wisdom & Guided Meditations to Strengthen & Calm Body, Heart, Mind & Spirit
By Rabbi Elie Kaplan Spitz Combines Jewish tradition, contemporary psychology and world spiritual writings with practical contemplative exercises to guide you to see the familiar in fresh new ways.
6 x 9, 208 pp, Quality PB, 978-1-58023-823-6 **$19.99**

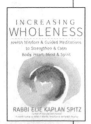

Living the Life of Jewish Meditation: A Comprehensive Guide to Practice and Experience *By Rabbi Yoel Glick*
Combines the knowledge of Judaism with the spiritual practice of Yoga to lead you to an encounter with your true self. Includes nineteen different meditations.
6 x 9, 272 pp, Quality PB, 978-1-58023-802-1 **$18.99**

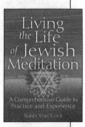

Mussar Yoga: Blending an Ancient Jewish Spiritual Practice with Yoga to Transform Body and Soul
By Edith R. Brotman, PhD, RYT-500; Foreword by Alan Morinis
A clear and easy-to-use introduction to an embodied spiritual practice for anyone seeking profound and lasting self-transformation.
7 x 9, 224 pp, 40+ b/w photos, Quality PB, 978-1-58023-784-0 **$18.99**

The Magic of Hebrew Chant: Healing the Spirit, Transforming the Mind, Deepening Love *By Rabbi Shefa Gold; Foreword by Sylvia Boorstein*
Introduces this transformative spiritual practice as a way to unlock the power of sacred texts and make prayer and meditation the delight of your life. Includes musical notations. 6 x 9, 352 pp, Quality PB, 978-1-58023-671-3 **$24.99**

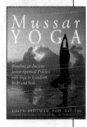

The Magic of Hebrew Chant Companion: The Big Book of Musical Notations and Incantations 8½ x 11, 154 pp, PB, 978-1-58023-722-2 **$19.99**

Aleph-Bet Yoga: Embodying the Hebrew Letters for Physical and Spiritual Well-Being
By Steven A. Rapp; Foreword by Tamar Frankiel, PhD, and Judy Greenfeld; Preface by Hart Lazer
7 x 10, 128 pp, b/w photos, Quality PB, Lay-flat binding, 978-1-58023-162-6 **$16.95**

Discovering Jewish Meditation, 2nd Edition
Instruction & Guidance for Learning an Ancient Spiritual Practice
By Nan Fink Gefen, PhD 6 x 9, 208 pp, Quality PB, 978-1-58023-462-7 **$16.99**

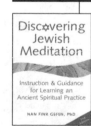

The Handbook of Jewish Meditation Practices
A Guide for Enriching the Sabbath and Other Days of Your Life
By Rabbi David A. Cooper 6 x 9, 208 pp, Quality PB, 978-1-58023-102-2 **$16.95**

Jewish Meditation Practices for Everyday Life: Awakening Your Heart, Connecting with God *By Rabbi Jeff Roth* 6 x 9, 224 pp, Quality PB, 978-1-58023-397-2 **$18.99**

Ritual / Sacred Practices

God in Your Body: Kabbalah, Mindfulness and Embodied Spiritual Practice
By Jay Michaelson 6 x 9, 272 pp, Quality PB, 978-1-58023-304-0 **$18.99**

Jewish Ritual: A Brief Introduction for Christians
By Rabbi Kerry M. Olitzky and Rabbi Daniel Judson
5½ x 8½, 144 pp, Quality PB, 978-1-58023-210-4 **$14.99**

The Rituals & Practices of a Jewish Life: A Handbook for Personal Spiritual Renewal
Edited by Rabbi Kerry M. Olitzky and Rabbi Daniel Judson
6 x 9, 272 pp, Illus., Quality PB, 978-1-58023-169-5 **$19.99**

The Sacred Art of Lovingkindness: Preparing to Practice
By Rabbi Rami Shapiro 5½ x 8½, 176 pp, Quality PB, 978-1-59473-151-8 **$16.99***

Mystery & Detective Fiction

Criminal Kabbalah: An Intriguing Anthology of Jewish Mystery & Detective Fiction
Edited by Lawrence W. Raphael; Foreword by Laurie R. King
6 x 9, 256 pp, Quality PB, 978-1-58023-109-1 **$16.95**

Mystery Midrash: An Anthology of Jewish Mystery & Detective Fiction
Edited by Lawrence W. Raphael; Preface by Joel Siegel
6 x 9, 304 pp, Quality PB, 978-1-58023-055-1 **$16.95**

*A book from SkyLight Paths, Jewish Lights' sister imprint

Holidays / Holy Days

Prayers of Awe Series

An exciting new series that examines the High Holy Day liturgy to enrich the praying experience of everyone—whether experienced worshipers or guests who encounter Jewish prayer for the very first time. *Edited by Rabbi Lawrence A. Hoffman, PhD*

Who by Fire, Who by Water—*Un'taneh Tokef*
6 x 9, 272 pp, Quality PB, 978-1-58023-672-0 **$19.99**; HC, 978-1-58023-424-5 **$24.99**

All These Vows—*Kol Nidre*
6 x 9, 288 pp, HC, 978-1-58023-430-6 **$24.99**

We Have Sinned—Sin and Confession in Judaism: *Ashamnu and Al Chet*
6 x 9, 304 pp, HC, 978-1-58023-612-6 **$24.99**

May God Remember: Memory and Memorializing in Judaism—*Yizkor*
6 x 9, 304 pp, HC, 978-1-58023-689-8 **$24.99**

All the World: Universalism, Particularism and the High Holy Days
6 x 9, 288 pp, HC, 978-1-58023-783-3 **$24.99**

Naming God

Avinu Malkeinu—Our Father, Our King
Edited by Rabbi Lawrence A. Hoffman, PhD

Almost forty contributors from the US, Israel, UK, Europe and Canada examine one of Judaism's favorite prayers and provide analysis of the age-old but altogether modern problem of naming God. 6 x 9, 336 pp, HC, 978-1-58023-817-5 **$27.99**

Rosh Hashanah Readings: Inspiration, Information and Contemplation
Yom Kippur Readings: Inspiration, Information and Contemplation
Edited by Rabbi Dov Peretz Elkins; Section Introductions from Arthur Green's These Are the Words
Rosh Hashanah: 6 x 9, 400 pp, Quality PB, 978-1-58023-437-5 **$19.99**
Yom Kippur: 6 x 9, 368 pp, Quality PB, 978-1-58023-438-2 **$19.99**; HC, 978-1-58023-271-5 **$24.99**

Shabbat, 2nd Edition: The Family Guide to Preparing for and Celebrating the Sabbath
By Dr. Ron Wolfson 7 x 9, 320 pp, Illus., Quality PB, 978-1-58023-164-0 **$21.99**

Hanukkah, 2nd Edition: The Family Guide to Spiritual Celebration
By Dr. Ron Wolfson 7 x 9, 240 pp, Illus., Quality PB, 978-1-58023-122-0 **$18.95**

Passover

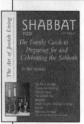

My People's Passover Haggadah

Traditional Texts, Modern Commentaries

Edited by Rabbi Lawrence A. Hoffman, PhD, and David Arnow, PhD

A diverse and exciting collection of commentaries on the traditional Passover Haggadah—in two volumes!
Vol. 1: 7 x 10, 304 pp, HC, 978-1-58023-354-5 **$24.99**
Vol. 2: 7 x 10, 320 pp, HC, 978-1-58023-346-0 **$24.99**

Creating Lively Passover Seders, 2nd Edition: A Sourcebook of Engaging Tales, Texts & Activities By David Arnow, PhD 7 x 9, 464 pp, Quality PB, 978-1-58023-444-3 **$24.99**

Freedom Journeys: The Tale of Exodus and Wilderness across Millennia
By Rabbi Arthur O. Waskow and Rabbi Phyllis O. Berman
6 x 9, 288 pp, HC, 978-1-58023-445-0 **$24.99**

Leading the Passover Journey: The Seder's Meaning Revealed, the Haggadah's Story Retold By Rabbi Nathan Laufer
6 x 9, 224 pp, Quality PB, 978-1-58023-399-6 **$18.99**

Passover, 2nd Edition: The Family Guide to Spiritual Celebration
By Dr. Ron Wolfson with Joel Lurie Grishaver 7 x 9, 416 pp, Quality PB, 978-1-58023-174-9 **$19.95**

The Women's Passover Companion: Women's Reflections on the Festival of Freedom
Edited by Rabbi Sharon Cohen Anisfeld, Tara Mohr and Catherine Spector
Foreword by Paula E. Hyman
6 x 9, 352 pp, Quality PB, 978-1-58023-231-9 **$19.99**; HC, 978-1-58023-128-2 **$24.95**

The Women's Seder Sourcebook: Rituals & Readings for Use at the Passover Seder
Edited by Rabbi Sharon Cohen Anisfeld, Tara Mohr and Catherine Spector
6 x 9, 384 pp, Quality PB, 978-1-58023-232-6 **$19.99**

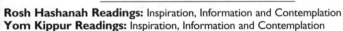

Social Justice

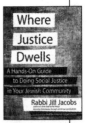

Where Justice Dwells
A Hands-On Guide to Doing Social Justice in Your Jewish Community
By Rabbi Jill Jacobs; Foreword by Rabbi David Saperstein
Provides ways to envision and act on your own ideals of social justice.
7 x 9, 288 pp, Quality PB, 978-1-58023-453-5 **$24.99**

There Shall Be No Needy
Pursuing Social Justice through Jewish Law and Tradition
By Rabbi Jill Jacobs; Foreword by Rabbi Elliot N. Dorff, PhD; Preface by Simon Greer
Confronts the most pressing issues of twenty-first-century America from a deeply
Jewish perspective. 6 x 9, 288 pp, Quality PB, 978-1-58023-425-2 **$16.99**
There Shall Be No Needy Teacher's Guide 8½ x 11, 56 pp, PB, 978-1-58023-429-0 **$8.99**

Conscience
The Duty to Obey and the Duty to Disobey
By Rabbi Harold M. Schulweis (z"l)
Examines the idea of conscience and the role conscience plays in our relationships
to government, law, ethics, religion, human nature, God—and to each other.
6 x 9, 160 pp, Quality PB, 978-1-58023-419-1 **$16.99**; HC, 978-1-58023-375-0 **$19.99**

Judaism and Justice: The Jewish Passion to Repair the World
By Rabbi Sidney Schwarz; Foreword by Ruth Messinger
6 x 9, 352 pp, Quality PB, 978-1-58023-353-8 **$19.99**

Spirituality / Women's Interest

Embracing the Divine Feminine: Finding God through the Ecstasy of
Physical Love—The Song of Songs Annotated & Explained
Annotation and Translation by Rabbi Rami Shapiro; Foreword by Rev. Cynthia Bourgeault, PhD
*Restores the Song of Songs' eroticism and interprets it as a celebration of the love between the
Divine Feminine and the contemporary spiritual seeker.*
5½ x 8½, 176 pp, Quality PB, 978-1-59473-575-2 **$16.99***

The Women's Haftarah Commentary
New Insights from Women Rabbis on the 54 Weekly Haftarah Portions,
the 5 Megillot & Special Shabbatot
Edited by Rabbi Elyse Goldstein
Illuminates the historical significance of female portrayals in the Haftarah and the
Five Megillot. 6 x 9, 560 pp, Quality PB, 978-1-58023-371-2 **$19.99**

The Women's Torah Commentary
New Insights from Women Rabbis on the 54 Weekly Torah Portions
Edited by Rabbi Elyse Goldstein
Over fifty women rabbis offer inspiring insights on the Torah, in a week-by-week format.
6 x 9, 496 pp, Quality PB, 978-1-58023-370-5 **$19.99**

The Divine Feminine in Biblical Wisdom Literature
Selections Annotated & Explained
Translation & Annotation by Rabbi Rami Shapiro; Foreword by Rev. Cynthia Bourgeault, PhD
5½ x 8½, 240 pp, Quality PB, 978-1-59473-109-9 **$18.99***

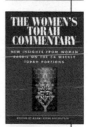

New Jewish Feminism: Probing the Past, Forging the Future
Edited by Rabbi Elyse Goldstein; Foreword by Anita Diamant
6 x 9, 480 pp, HC, 978-1-58023-359-0 **$24.99**

The Quotable Jewish Woman
Wisdom, Inspiration & Humor from the Mind & Heart
Edited by Elaine Bernstein Partnow
6 x 9, 496 pp, Quality PB, 978-1-58023-236-4 **$19.99**

See *Passover* for *The Women's Passover Companion: Women's Reflections on the
Festival of Freedom* and *The Women's Seder Sourcebook: Rituals & Readings for Use
at the Passover Seder.*

*A book from SkyLight Paths, Jewish Lights' sister imprint

Inspiration

The Best Boy in the United States of America
A Memoir of Blessings and Kisses *By Dr. Ron Wolfson*
Will resonate with anyone seeking to shape stronger families and communities and live a life of joy and purpose. 6 x 9, 192 pp, HC, 978-1-58023-838-0 **$19.99**

The Chutzpah Imperative: Empowering Today's Jews for a Life
That Matters *By Rabbi Edward Feinstein; Foreword by Rabbi Laura Geller*
A new view of chutzpah as Jewish self-empowerment to be God's partner and repair the world. Reveals Judaism's ancient message, its deepest purpose and most precious treasures. 6 x 9, 192 pp, HC, 978-1-58023-792-5 **$21.99**

Judaism's Ten Best Ideas: A Brief Guide for Seekers
By Rabbi Arthur Green, PhD A highly accessible introduction to Judaism's greatest contributions to civilization, drawing on Jewish mystical tradition and the author's experience. 4½ x 6½, 112 pp, Quality PB, 978-1-58023-803-8 **$9.99**

The Empty Chair: Finding Hope and Joy—Timeless Wisdom from a Hasidic Master,
Rebbe Nachman of Breslov *Adapted by Moshe Mykoff and the Breslov Research Institute*
4 x 6, 128 pp, Deluxe PB w/ flaps, 978-1-879045-67-5 **$9.99**

The Gentle Weapon: Prayers for Everyday and Not-So-Everyday Moments—
Timeless Wisdom from the Teachings of the Hasidic Master Rebbe Nachman of Breslov
Adapted by Moshe Mykoff and S. C. Mizrahi, together with the Breslov Research Institute
4 x 6, 144 pp, Deluxe PB w/ flaps, 978-1-58023-022-3 **$9.99**

God Whispers: Stories of the Soul, Lessons of the Heart *By Rabbi Karyn D. Kedar*
6 x 9, 176 pp, Quality PB, 978-1-58023-088-9 **$16.99**

God's To-Do List: 103 Ways to Be an Angel and Do God's Work on Earth
By Dr. Ron Wolfson 6 x 9, 144 pp, Quality PB, 978-1-58023-301-9 **$16.99**

Happiness and the Human Spirit: The Spirituality of Becoming the Best You Can Be
By Rabbi Abraham J. Twerski, MD
6 x 9, 176 pp, Quality PB, 978-1-58023-404-7 **$16.99**; HC, 978-1-58023-343-9 **$19.99**

Life's Daily Blessings: Inspiring Reflections on Gratitude and Joy for Every Day,
Based on Jewish Wisdom *By Rabbi Kerry M. Olitzky*
4½ x 6½, 368 pp, Quality PB, 978-1-58023-396-5 **$16.99**

Sacred Intentions: Morning Inspiration to Strengthen the Spirit, Based on Jewish Wisdom
By Rabbi Kerry M. Olitzky and Rabbi Lori Forman-Jacobi
4½ x 6½, 448 pp, Quality PB, 978-1-58023-061-2 **$16.99**

The Seven Questions You're Asked in Heaven: Reviewing and Renewing Your
Life on Earth *By Dr. Ron Wolfson* 6 x 9, 176 pp, Quality PB, 978-1-58023-407-8 **$16.99**

Kabbalah / Mysticism

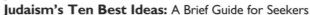

Walking the Path of the Jewish Mystic: How to Expand Your
Awareness and Transform Your Life *By Rabbi Yoel Glick*
A unique guide to the nature of both physical and spiritual reality.
6 x 9, 224 pp, Quality PB, 978-1-58023-843-4 **$18.99**

Ehyeh: A Kabbalah for Tomorrow
By Rabbi Arthur Green, PhD 6 x 9, 224 pp, Quality PB, 978-1-58023-213-5 **$18.99**

The Gift of Kabbalah: Discovering the Secrets of Heaven, Renewing Your Life on Earth
By Tamar Frankiel, PhD 6 x 9, 256 pp, Quality PB, 978-1-58023-141-1 **$18.99**

Jewish Mysticism and the Spiritual Life: Classical Texts, Contemporary
Reflections *Edited by Dr. Lawrence Fine, Dr. Eitan Fishbane and Rabbi Or N. Rose*
6 x 9, 256 pp, Quality PB, 978-1-58023-719-2 **$18.99**

Seek My Face: A Jewish Mystical Theology *By Rabbi Arthur Green, PhD*
6 x 9, 304 pp, Quality PB, 978-1-58023-130-5 **$19.95**

Zohar: Annotated & Explained *Translation & Annotation by Dr. Daniel C. Matt*
Foreword by Andrew Harvey 5½ x 8½, 176 pp, Quality PB, 978-1-893361-51-5 **$18.99**
(A book from SkyLight Paths, Jewish Lights' sister imprint)

Spirituality / Prayer

Davening: A Guide to Meaningful Jewish Prayer
By Rabbi Zalman Schachter-Shalomi (z"l) with Joel Segel; Foreword by Rabbi Lawrence Kushner
A fresh approach to prayer for all who wish to appreciate the power of prayer's poetry, song and ritual, and to join the age-old conversation that Jews have had with God.   6 x 9, 240 pp, Quality PB, 978-1-58023-627-0 **$18.99**

Jewish Men Pray: Words of Yearning, Praise, Petition, Gratitude and Wonder from Traditional and Contemporary Sources
Edited by Rabbi Kerry M. Olitzky and Stuart M. Matlins; Foreword by Rabbi Bradley Shavit Artson, DHL
A celebration of Jewish men's voices in prayer—to strengthen, heal, comfort, and inspire—from the ancient world up to our own day.
5 x 7¼, 400 pp, HC, 978-1-58023-628-7 **$19.99**

Making Prayer Real: Leading Jewish Spiritual Voices on Why Prayer Is Difficult and What to Do about It   *By Rabbi Mike Comins*   6 x 9, 320 pp, Quality PB, 978-1-58023-417-7 **$18.99**

Witnesses to the One: The Spiritual History of the *Sh'ma*
By Rabbi Joseph B. Meszler; Foreword by Rabbi Elyse Goldstein
6 x 9, 176 pp, Quality PB, 978-1-58023-400-9 **$16.99**; HC, 978-1-58023-309-5 **$19.99**

My People's Prayer Book Series: Traditional Prayers, Modern
Commentaries   *Edited by Rabbi Lawrence A. Hoffman, PhD*
Provides diverse and exciting commentary to the traditional liturgy. Will help you find new wisdom in Jewish prayer, and bring liturgy into your life. Each book includes Hebrew text, modern translations and commentaries from all perspectives of the Jewish world.

Vol. 1—The *Sh'ma* and Its Blessings
  7 x 10, 168 pp, HC, 978-1-879045-79-8 **$29.99**
Vol. 2—The *Amidah*   7 x 10, 240 pp, HC, 978-1-879045-80-4 **$29.99**
Vol. 3—*P'sukei D'zimrah* (Morning Psalms)
  7 x 10, 240 pp, HC, 978-1-879045-81-1 **$35.00**
Vol. 4—*Seder K'riat Hatorah* (The Torah Service)
  7 x 10, 264 pp, HC, 978-1-879045-82-8 **$29.99**
Vol. 5—*Birkhot Hashachar* (Morning Blessings)
  7 x 10, 240 pp, HC, 978-1-879045-83-5 **$35.00**
Vol. 6—*Tachanun* and Concluding Prayers
  7 x 10, 240 pp, HC, 978-1-879045-84-2 **$24.95**
Vol. 7—Shabbat at Home   7 x 10, 240 pp, HC, 978-1-879045-85-9 **$29.99**
Vol. 8—*Kabbalat Shabbat* (Welcoming Shabbat in the Synagogue)
  7 x 10, 240 pp, HC, 978-1-58023-121-3 **$24.99**
Vol. 9—Welcoming the Night: *Minchah* and *Ma'ariv* (Afternoon and
  Evening Prayer)   7 x 10, 272 pp, HC, 978-1-58023-262-3 **$35.00**
Vol. 10—Shabbat Morning: *Shacharit* and *Musaf* (Morning and
  Additional Services)   7 x 10, 240 pp, HC, 978-1-58023-240-1 **$35.00**

Spirituality / Lawrence Kushner

I'm God; You're Not: Observations on Organized Religion & Other Disguises of the Ego
6 x 9, 256 pp, Quality PB, 978-1-58023-513-6 **$18.99**; HC, 978-1-58023-441-2 **$21.99**

The Book of Letters: A Mystical Hebrew Alphabet
Popular HC Edition   6 x 9, 80 pp, 2-color text, 978-1-879045-00-2 **$24.95**
Collector's Limited Edition   9 x 12, 80 pp, gold-foil-embossed pages, w/ limited-edition silk-screened print, 978-1-879045-04-0 **$349.00**

The Book of Miracles: A Young Person's Guide to Jewish Spiritual Awareness
6 x 9, 96 pp, 2-color illus., HC, 978-1-879045-78-1 **$16.95** *For ages 9–13*

God Was in This Place & I, i Did Not Know: Finding Self, Spirituality and
Ultimate Meaning   6 x 9, 192 pp, Quality PB, 978-1-879045-33-0 **$18.99**

Honey from the Rock: An Introduction to Jewish Mysticism
6 x 9, 176 pp, Quality PB, 978-1-58023-073-5 **$18.99**

Invisible Lines of Connection: Sacred Stories of the Ordinary
5½ x 8½, 160 pp, Quality PB, 978-1-879045-98-9 **$16.99**

The Way Into Jewish Mystical Tradition
6 x 9, 224 pp, Quality PB, 978-1-58023-200-5 **$18.99**

Spirituality

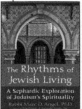

The Rhythms of Jewish Living
A Sephardic Exploration of Judaism's Spirituality
By Rabbi Marc D. Angel, PhD Reclaims the natural, balanced and insightful teachings of Sephardic Judaism that can and should imbue modern Jewish spirituality.
6 x 9, 208 pp, Quality PB, 978-1-58023-834-2 **$18.99**

God and the Big Bang, 2nd Edition
Discovering Harmony between Science and Spirituality
By Daniel C. Matt Updated and expanded. Draws on the insights of physics and Kabbalah to uncover the sense of wonder and oneness that connects humankind with the universe and God.   6 x 9, 224 pp, Quality PB, 978-1-58023-836-6 **$18.99**

Amazing Chesed: Living a Grace-Filled Judaism
By Rabbi Rami Shapiro Drawing from ancient and contemporary, traditional and non-traditional Jewish wisdom, reclaims the idea of grace in Judaism.
6 x 9, 176 pp, Quality PB, 978-1-58023-624-9 **$16.99**

Perennial Wisdom for the Spiritually Independent: Sacred Teachings—

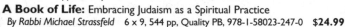

Annotated & Explained *Annotation by Rabbi Rami Shapiro; Foreword by Richard Rohr* Weaves sacred texts and teachings from the world's major religions into a coherent exploration of the five core questions at the heart of every religion's search.
5½ x 8½, 336 pp, Quality PB, 978-1-59473-515-8 **$16.99***

A Book of Life: Embracing Judaism as a Spiritual Practice
By Rabbi Michael Strassfeld   6 x 9, 544 pp, Quality PB, 978-1-58023-247-0 **$24.99**

Bringing the Psalms to Life: How to Understand and Use the Book of Psalms
By Rabbi Daniel F. Polish, PhD   6 x 9, 208 pp, Quality PB, 978-1-58023-157-2 **$18.99**

Does the Soul Survive? 2nd Edition: A Jewish Journey to Belief in Afterlife, Past Lives & Living with Purpose *By Rabbi Elie Kaplan Spitz; Foreword by Brian L. Weiss, MD*
6 x 9, 288 pp, Quality PB, 978-1-58023-818-2 **$18.99**

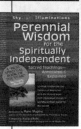

First Steps to a New Jewish Spirit: Reb Zalman's Guide to Recapturing the Intimacy & Ecstasy in Your Relationship with God *By Rabbi Zalman Schachter-Shalomi (z"l) with Donald Gropman*
6 x 9, 144 pp, Quality PB, 978-1-58023-182-4 **$16.95**

Foundations of Sephardic Spirituality: The Inner Life of Jews of the Ottoman Empire
By Rabbi Marc D. Angel, PhD   6 x 9, 224 pp, Quality PB, 978-1-58023-341-5 **$18.99**

The God Upgrade: Finding Your 21st-Century Spirituality in Judaism's 5,000-Year-Old Tradition *By Rabbi Jamie Korngold; Foreword by Rabbi Harold M. Schulweis*
6 x 9, 176 pp, Quality PB, 978-1-58023-443-6 **$15.99**

The Jewish Lights Spirituality Handbook: A Guide to Understanding, Exploring & Living a Spiritual Life *Edited by Stuart M. Matlins*
6 x 9, 456 pp, Quality PB, 978-1-58023-093-3 **$19.99**

Jewish with Feeling: A Guide to Meaningful Jewish Practice
By Rabbi Zalman Schachter-Shalomi (z"l) with Joel Segel
5½ x 8½, 288 pp, Quality PB, 978-1-58023-691-1 **$19.99**

Judaism, Physics and God: Searching for Sacred Metaphors in a Post-Einstein World
By Rabbi David W. Nelson
6 x 9, 352 pp, Quality PB, inc. reader's discussion guide, 978-1-58023-306-4 **$18.99**
HC, 352 pp, 978-1-58023-252-4 **$24.99**

Repentance: The Meaning and Practice of Teshuvah
By Dr. Louis E. Newman; Foreword by Rabbi Harold M. Schulweis; Preface by Rabbi Karyn D. Kedar
6 x 9, 256 pp, Quality PB, 978-1-58023-718-5 **$18.99**

Tanya, the Masterpiece of Hasidic Wisdom: Selections Annotated & Explained
Translation & Annotation by Rabbi Rami Shapiro; Foreword by Rabbi Zalman Schachter-Shalomi (z"l)
5½ x 8½, 240 pp, Quality PB, 978-1-59473-275-1 **$18.99***

These Are the Words, 2nd Edition: A Vocabulary of Jewish Spiritual Life
By Rabbi Arthur Green, PhD   6 x 9, 320 pp, Quality PB, 978-1-58023-494-8 **$19.99**

Your Word Is Fire: The Hasidic Masters on Contemplative Prayer
Edited and translated by Rabbi Arthur Green, PhD, and Barry W. Holtz
6 x 9, 160 pp, Quality PB, 978-1-879045-25-5 **$16.99**

*A book from SkyLight Paths, Jewish Lights' sister imprint

Congregation Resources

Disaster Spiritual Care, 2nd Edition
Practical Clergy Responses to Community, Regional and National Tragedy
Edited by Rabbi Stephen B. Roberts, BCJC, and Rev. Willard W. C. Ashley Sr., DMin, DH
Updated and expanded—the definitive guidebook for counseling not only the victims of disaster but also the clergy and caregivers who are called to service in the wake of a crisis. 6 x 9, 384 pp (est), HC, 978-1-59473-587-5 **$50.00***

Jewish Ethical Values: A Sourcebook of Classic Texts and Their Practical Uses for Our Lives *By Dr. Byron L. Sherwin and Dr. Seymour J. Cohen*
Offers selections from classic Jewish ethical literature and clear explanations of their historic context of each writing and thoughtful applications of their wisdom for our lives today. 6 x 9, 336 pp, Quality PB, 978-1-58023-835-9 **$19.99**

New Membership & Financial Alternatives for the American Synagogue From Traditional Dues to Fair Share to Gifts from the Heart
*By Rabbi Kerry M. Olitzky and Rabbi Avi S. Olitzky; Foreword by Dr. Ron Wolfson
Afterword by Rabbi Dan Judson* Practice values-driven ways to make changes to open wide the synagogue doors to many. 6 x 9, 208 pp, Quality PB, 978-1-58023-820-5 **$19.99**

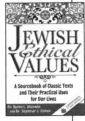

Relational Judaism: Using the Power of Relationships to Transform the Jewish Community *By Dr. Ron Wolfson* How to transform the model of twentieth-century Jewish institutions into twenty-first-century relational communities offering meaning and purpose, belonging and blessing.
6 x 9, 288 pp, HC, 978-1-58023-666-9 **$24.99**

The Spirituality of Welcoming: How to Transform Your Congregation into a Sacred Community *By Dr. Ron Wolfson*
Shows crucial hospitality is for congregational survival and dives into the practicalities of cultivating openness.
6 x 9, 224 pp, Quality PB, 978-1-58023-244-9 **$19.99**

Jewish Megatrends: Charting the Course of the American Jewish Future
By Rabbi Sidney Schwarz; Foreword by Ambassador Stuart E. Eizenstat
Visionary solutions for a community ripe for transformational change—from fourteen leading innovators of Jewish life. 6 x 9, 288 pp, HC, 978-1-58023-667-6 **$24.99**

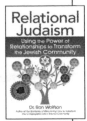

Building a Successful Volunteer Culture: Finding Meaning in Service in the Jewish Community *By Rabbi Charles Simon; Foreword by Shelley Lindauer; Preface by Dr. Ron Wolfson*
6 x 9, 192 pp, Quality PB, 978-1-58023-408-5 **$16.99**

Empowered Judaism: What Independent Minyanim Can Teach Us about Building Vibrant Jewish Communities *By Rabbi Elie Kaunfer; Foreword by Prof. Jonathan D. Sarna*
6 x 9, 224 pp, Quality PB, 978-1-58023-412-2 **$18.99**

Inspired Jewish Leadership: Practical Approaches to Building Strong Communities
By Dr. Erica Brown 6 x 9, 256 pp, HC, 978-1-58023-361-3 **$27.99**

Judaism and Health: A Handbook of Practical, Professional and Scholarly Resources
*Edited by Jeff Levin, PhD, MPH, and Michele F. Prince, LCSW, MAJCS
Foreword by Rabbi Elliot N. Dorff, PhD* 6 x 9, 448 pp, HC, 978-1-58023-714-7 **$50.00**

Jewish Pastoral Care, 2nd Edition: A Practical Handbook from Traditional & Contemporary Sources *Edited by Rabbi Dayle A. Friedman, MSW, MA, BCC*
6 x 9, 528 pp, Quality PB, 978-1-58023-427-6 **$35.00**

A Practical Guide to Rabbinic Counseling
Edited by Rabbi Yisrael N. Levitz, PhD, and Rabbi Abraham J. Twerski, MD
6 x 9, 432 pp, HC, 978-1-58023-562-4 **$40.00**

Professional Spiritual & Pastoral Care: A Practical Clergy and Chaplain's Handbook
Edited by Rabbi Stephen B. Roberts, MBA, MHL, BCJC 6 x 9, 480 pp, HC, 978-1-59473-312-3 **$50.00***

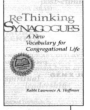

Reimagining Leadership in Jewish Organizations: Ten Practical Lessons to Help You Implement Change and Achieve Your Goals
By Dr. Misha Galperin 6 x 9, 192 pp, Quality PB, 978-1-58023-492-4 **$16.99**

Rethinking Synagogues: A New Vocabulary for Congregational Life
By Rabbi Lawrence A. Hoffman, PhD 6 x 9, 240 pp, Quality PB, 978-1-58023-248-7 **$19.99**

*A book from SkyLight Paths, Jewish Lights' sister imprint

About Jewish Lights

People of all faiths and backgrounds yearn for books that attract, engage, educate, and spiritually inspire.

Our principal goal is to stimulate thought and help all people learn about who the Jewish People are, where they come from, and what the future can be made to hold. While people of our diverse Jewish heritage are the primary audience, our books speak to people in the Christian world as well and will broaden their understanding of Judaism and the roots of their own faith.

We bring to you authors who are at the forefront of spiritual thought and experience. While each has something different to say, they all say it in a voice that you can hear.

Our books are designed to welcome you and then to engage, stimulate, and inspire. We judge our success not only by whether or not our books are beautiful and commercially successful, but by whether or not they make a difference in your life.

For your information and convenience, at the back of this book we have provided a list of other Jewish Lights books you might find interesting and useful. They cover all the categories of your life:

Bar/Bat Mitzvah	Life Cycle
Bible Study / Midrash	Meditation
Children's Books	Men's Interest
Congregation Resources	Parenting
Current Events / History	Prayer / Ritual / Sacred Practice
Ecology / Environment	Social Justice
Fiction: Mystery, Science Fiction	Spirituality
Grief / Healing	Theology / Philosophy
Holidays / Holy Days	Travel
Inspiration	Twelve Steps
Kabbalah / Mysticism / Enneagram	Women's Interest

Stuart M. Matlins, Publisher

Or phone, fax, mail or email to: **JEWISH LIGHTS Publishing**
Sunset Farm Offices, Route 4 • P.O. Box 237 • Woodstock, Vermont 05091
Tel: (802) 457-4000 • Fax: (802) 457-4004 • www.jewishlights.com
Credit card orders: **(800) 962-4544** (8:30AM–5:30PM EST Monday–Friday)
Generous discounts on quantity orders. SATISFACTION GUARANTEED. Prices subject to change.

For more information about each book, visit our website at www.jewishlights.com.